Making a Difference

Personal Essays by Today's College Teachers

TOWNSEND PRESS   Marlton, NJ 08053

To all those who help students learn

Townsend Press, Inc.
Pavilions at Greentree—408
Marlton, NJ 08053

Ordering information:

Individuals may order *Making a Difference*
for $5.00 per book ($3.00 for the book; $2.00
for shipping costs). Send a check or money order
(payable to Townsend Press) to the address below.

Bookstores may order the book for $3.00 net plus
shipping costs.

Send book orders to:

Townsend Press
1038 Industrial Drive
West Berlin, New Jersey 08091

For even faster service, call us at our toll-free number:
1-800-772-6410

Or FAX your request to:
1-609-753-0649

ISBN 0-944210-99-6

Contents

Preface

The personal essays in *Making a Difference* were selected from the winning entries in two separate Townsend Press writing contests for developmental teachers. These essays, by teachers across the country, were written in response to the following topics:

- What Made Me Decide to Be a Teacher
- The Most Influential Teacher I Ever Had
- How I Learned to Teach
- The Pleasures and/or Pains of Teaching
- The Comic Side of Teaching
- My Most Fulfilling Experience as a Teacher
- My Most Unforgettable Student
- What Students Have Taught Me
- My Personal Advice to New Developmental Teachers
- How I Energize the Developmental Education Classroom
- My Most Successful Assignment(s)
- Why I Would Decide to Teach Again
- Lessons I Never Learned in School

Entrants were required to be part- or full-time teachers at a two-or four-year college and to be teaching a developmental reading, writing, or ESL course within one year of submitting an entry.

The essays in this book are representative of the hundreds of often moving pieces that we received—rich, loving, and passionate accounts by writers for whom teaching is not just a job but the most meaningful of professions. The essays remind us of what we already know but tend, in the course of busy and sometimes frustrating days in the classroom, to forget: that helping students learn carries its own intrinsic rewards; that making a difference in another person's life can be a source of real joy.

Some essays celebrate an admired instructor who was a role model even before the writer entered the teaching profession. One instructor writes:

- What did we learn? You taught us how to read like explorers, using our minds like tools; whether they were bulldozers, or spades, we were all in it together; digging, searching, experiencing language and literature in worlds long ago. . . . Words became our friends, our companions. We learned to respect words and use them carefully, judiciously. We learned to love words and use them playfully, joyously. I think we learned most of all that learning can be fun.

  Learning was fun in your class because your energy and enthusiasm virtually filled the room. It didn't matter if we were diagramming sentences or reading Shakespeare; you seemed electric with excitement when you stood in front of the classroom. I sat in the front row, and you know what? I got CHARGED! Otherwise shy and unsure of myself, in your classroom I had a barracuda-like belief in myself. I believed I could accomplish great things with the English language. . . . I believed I could be "somebody" someday. I believed, somehow I knew, I would carry what I learned in that classroom with me for the rest of my life. So far, I have.

For another instructor, homebound while recovering from a childhood bout with rheumatic fever, a visiting teacher unlocks the secret of the learning process:

- Without using educational jargon, Mrs. Schultz explained to me many of the facets of good teaching as we watched the smaller of the two baby birds struggle to keep up with his sibling. On one particular day, an especially fierce Canadian wind blew over my house from nearby Lake Ontario. Facing into the wind, the tiny baby could barely stay upright on the telephone wire, where his mother had left him while she escorted her other baby to a nearby cherry tree.

  "See how she flies ahead showing the way, but then circles back behind, chirping and urging the chick toward her goal?" Mrs. Schultz remarked admiringly.

  Suddenly the wind was too much for the little bird left clinging to the telephone wire. He swung around nearly in a circle. The mother bird headed back to him, chirping what we imagined to be "Hang on! Just hang on that wire!" By the time she returned, he was upright again, but clearly terrified. She perched next to him and chirped comfortingly at him, but then she began to urge him out into the wind with her. Usually, she brought the stronger chick back to the wire before setting out with the weaker chick. This time, though, she must have decided that he needed to brave the wind immediately before another sharp gust blew away the remnants of his confidence.

  "She will take him to the maple tree. It's closer than the cherry tree. She wants to give him a taste of success. Then they will rest and move on to the cherry tree," Mrs. Schultz predicted.

Of course, she was right. Short-term, achievable goals; positive reinforcement; frequent practice and feedback; and expert and peer modeling were strategies that Mrs. Schultz and the mother robin knew instinctively. I, on the other hand, was not as gifted. I never understood the power of these simple teaching strategies until the mid-1960's when [my psychology professor] gave them labels and discussed them as part of our study of learning processes. . . . Even later, in the mid-1980's when I was President of the National Association for Developmental Education, my speeches before professional groups often began or ended with the robin's flight lessons as an analogy for effective developmental instruction; but I never acknowledged that my favorite analogy really belonged to my second-grade teacher or that I had been her developmental student.

Some essays share insights into the learning process that result from work with students. For example, one instructor reacts to a student paper on "Growing Potatoes." The student writes:

- *Potatoes grow underground. You can't really see what you've got unless you take the trouble to dig it up.*

The instructor responds:

That's what it's like teaching in a community college. Each semester begins with a sense of excitement that is tempered by apprehension because I know much of what I have to work with remains buried. Ryan's love for poetry is buried under his contempt for teachers. Karen's strength to defend her ideas in an essay lies buried under years of abuse. . . . There was much to be cultivated. . . .

The student continues:

We give some of the potatoes away. People cut them into pieces that include eyes and replant them. Then they grow again somewhere else.

The instructor concludes:

These are the secret rewards of teaching in a community college. The effects of what we do often remain hidden from us. Yes, we sometimes hear what happens after our students leave us. In the mail I've received first "real" paycheck stubs with smiley faces drawn on them and invitations to graduations from four-year colleges. One developmental student even went on to be nominated for a Michigan Press Award. But mostly the healthy roots spread in silent ways that we never hear about. Parents become positive role models for their children or other family members. Cycles of failure get broken. Students, once content with low-paying, unfulfilling jobs, begin to want more, which means they find the courage to face rejection instead of letting it control them. And eventually things begin to happen.

Other essays offer solid, practical advice to teachers of developmental studies:

- Never allow yourself to feel condescending toward students simply because they are working with material that you consider elementary. Put yourself in your student's position by imagining yourself taking the equivalent of a developmental-level course in some subject you find intimidating—whether that's auto repair, computer science, Japanese, calculus, chemistry, accounting, or whatever. Picture yourself summoning the courage to break through your fears and mental blocks and go to school, when you could have been sitting at home watching TV, and then being confronted by a sneering instructor who can't believe there's anyone who doesn't already know the basic stuff of that course's material. To exhibit such condescension would be not only cruel and immoral, but also unproductive and distracting to your students, so by condescending you would become a mediocre teacher, and then everyone else could condescend to you! Consider too the possibility that some of your students may already have mastered many of the subjects that intimidate you, so as soon as they've learned what you know in your field, they'll be way ahead of you overall.

But the most common recurring theme in *Making a Difference* is the students themselves. Over and over, teachers praise their students' achievements, which often come only after months (if not years) of effort and despite obstacles that would daunt many of us on the other side of the desk:

- My students live in what is essentially a third-world country. They have little money and therefore few choices. They have been in and out of emergency rooms, but few ever visit a doctor or a dentist. They have been to a lot of funerals; everyone knows somebody who was murdered, somebody killed in an automobile crash, somebody who committed suicide. They work long hours at minimum wage, minimum satisfaction, jobs just to keep their wretched cars running, cars they occasionally live in. They have survived child abuse of every kind. They have been humiliated in school. They are surrounded by violence—violence is the normal way of doing things. They know about divorce and alcoholism and drug abuse from the inside, from inside their own families. Prostitutes walk their streets. . . .

  My students should be basket cases, and much of their cohort is. We have the national statistics to prove it. But here they are in my classroom, incredibly generous of spirit. Nobody sneezes without a chorus of "God bless you." When a classmate does well, they break into applause. When someone needs assistance, they sacrifice their own performance to help. They hold open doors for perfectly healthy people at the other end of the corridor. They create little communities in a hostile world.

- I've often wondered why [my disabled students] fare so well in the face of their special challenges. Why were they able to rise above their difficulties and not be grounded by life's storms? I knew they all worked harder than the average student, learned to compensate for their lack, and practiced the art of filtering out the unimportant. But I felt it was something more that made them exceptional. After observing them for a long time, I concluded that they've done what the old Chinese proverb suggests: "If you can't change your fate, change your attitude."

They simply chose an attitude and went ahead with their lives. Their attitudes—persistence, optimism, excitement, tenacity, humor, appreciation, and hope—helped them soar and find a new perspective. They found freedom in looking down from above. Their problems diminished the higher they rose, so that their predicaments became not weights, but wings.

When I feel weighted down by my own disability—the grind of day-to-day living—I think of Mack or David or Spencer or Shannon and the things they taught me—and my own chair sprouts wings and takes flight.

We think you will find, as we did, that reading these essays is a rich and rewarding experience that will increase your pride in the difficult job you do every day. One of the contest winners writes that "sometimes I feel like a hero in this job, someone with character who is saving the day. More often, I feel like I'm surrounded by heroes. Either way, it's a pretty good way to feel." And another reminds us:

- Young teachers often feel that they get stuck with developmental courses which no one else wants. We "seasoned travelers" know that the students in these classes bring with them a wisdom about life's potential for disaster, a strong desire for information, a surprisingly intense camaraderie and willingness to share, and a deep respect for education. They are a gift to us all. They are why we go on being teachers.

The Editors

My Most Unforgettable Student
Philip Singleton, Towson State University

I remember Saa Nane—Eight O'Clock Island, jutting grey and stark from the still waters of Lake Victoria in the pink calm of an African sunrise. The train pulled slowly along Mwanza Sound on the final part of its thousand-mile journey from the Tanzanian coast. I leaned from the window of the dusty carriage to catch the warmth of the morning breeze. Small boys, barefoot and poorly clad, raced beside the track with metal trays of bananas, fried cassava, and whistles carved from the thin necks of gourds. There were women, faggots of dry brush on their heads, waving in silhouette against the bright reflection as the wheels ground to a slow halt in Mwanza station. On the platform the boys were shouting now, jostling for position and waving their goods in the faces of travelers and townsfolk. I stepped down into the milling crowd which swelled around me as the train emptied of warm bodies swathed in rainbow cotton, and Luogo was there to take my hand and pull me through the pressing throng to where the school truck waited in the dawning light of a cloudless day.

"*Hujambo!*" I said, "*Habari gani?*" What's the news?

"*Nzuri!*" Good. Even in the worst of times the news was good in Swahili.

"*Tutaenda sasa,*" he said. We will go now. I nodded and climbed aboard the truck, an old green Bedford with frayed tires and one door tied shut with wire. I sat on my rucksack among the ropes and burlap in the back. Luogo, as befitted a headmaster, rode in the cab with the driver as we bounced over the potholes of the town roads. At the roundabout, outside the party headquarters, the road was smooth and well kept, but soon afterwards the asphalt gave way and the truck jolted over the corrugated brown earth of a murram road. There were soil-brick huts to either side, some thatched, some with roofs of beaten tin. Among the huts were palm trees, kapok, and jacaranda laden with flowers of powder-blue. Smoke rose from cooking fires where old women stirred the thin ugali porridge, or fried rice cakes in cauldrons of hot, spitting oil. Men sat in the shade, talking and fanning at flies.

And everywhere were children, chasing the truck until they were lost in the rising clouds of dust, kicking a rag ball over the beaten earth, shouting and waving and grinning at the white man, the Mzungu, who stood and waved back, a foolish smile breaking on his own, amazed features.

I was 22 when I came to Mwanza, a VSO recruit seeking travel and adventure as a volunteer teacher in Tanzania. It was my first teaching job, far from home and in a culture more foreign than I could ever imagine. I rode the train north from Dar es Salaam armed with two months of teaching practice in a Liverpool comprehensive, a six-week language course in Kiswahili, and all the callow confidence of youth. My head was filled with images from old maps and geography books, pictures of animals grazing the wide savannah and tall Masai tending cattle on the dry plains. Here was African socialism, Nyrere's great experiments in village collectivism and self-reliance, a chance to make a difference in a land eternally poor. As a British-trained language teacher working for local wages in a third world country, I felt sure I had something to offer. Perhaps I did. But on that brilliant morning long ago, as the truck pulled down the sharp decline that led to the white school by the lakeshore, my heart swelling with the excitement of the unknown, I was not to know that in truth, I had as much to learn as any of my future students.

The school was old, built by the British fifty years before and decaying slowly in the years since independence. The white paint was flaking everywhere and the earth crept up the walls in stains of rusty red. The main buildings were arranged around a square courtyard, lit on my arrival by the crimson fire of a flame tree in full bloom. Outside the offices, the teachers waited in a formal line, eight Africans, each from a different tribe. Balingilaiki was the Head of English. He was a Haya from across the lake, tall and thin with a broad smile and shiny black skin. I shook his hand and those of the others, one by one. They greeted me in English, a gesture of respect and a way to prove to me their education. I was struck by how poor their clothes looked, threadbare safari suits, faded and worn. Luogo dismissed them with a wave. He took my hand and guided me on a tour of the school.

"We are happy today," he said. "You are needed. It is good that you are here."

I smiled and nodded. I felt happy to be wanted, to have expertise that could make a difference. It was nine o'clock now, but the classrooms were still empty. A few boys swept at the earth with small branches or carried water from the lake in tin cans swung between them from a wooden yoke. They stared at me and grinned. Past the school shop, boarded up and locked behind the 'Fanta' sign, dormitories were arranged in neat rows up the hillside. Each was named for an African leader. The one we approached was

"Sekou Toure." Outside, a boy swept at the earth, the slow swathes of the branch quickening as we came closer. Luogo made a brief, downward curl of the fingers, beckoning him to come near. The boy came slowly, his eyes cast down, hands clenched behind his back. He was thin, I remember, perhaps fifteen years old, his bony knees seeming too big for his long, spindly legs. His skin was satin-smooth and his hair shaved close. He wore the white shirt and cotton khaki shorts that were the uniform of Bwiru Boys'. On his feet were sandals made from strips of inner tube, nailed crosswise over pieces cut from the tread of old truck tires.

"*Shikamu,*" he said. Greetings, sir. His voice was a whisper.

"*Unafanya nini?*" replied Luogo. What are you doing? Luogo's voice was harsh. It struck me that he was showing his power, asserting discipline for discipline's sake.

"*Ninafanya kazi.*" I am working.

"*Ufanya upezi! Ufaya sasa!*" Do it quick! Do it now!

The boy thrashed at the earth with his switch and Luogo pulled at my hand. I held back and spoke to the boy in English.

"What's your name?"

He continued to sweep, his eyes still fixed on the red dust. He gave no reply.

"*Jina lako nane?*" The sweeping went on.

"*Habari,* John Samuel!"

"*Nzuri, nzuri sana!*"

He returned my greeting as we turned to climb the crumbling steps between the dormitories. We had taken several paces, Luogo still holding tight to my hand, when behind us I heard the low whisper of his voice above the swishing of the dust.

"*Karibu,*" he said. Welcome.

"*Asante.*" Thank you. Our eyes met and for a moment we exchanged the briefest of smiles before I turned again and followed Luogo upwards towards the long building under the high rocks, where the vervet monkeys chattered and fought in the growing warmth of morning.

It is not for our first meeting that I remember John Samuel, though the moment is clear in my mind in the distance of the passing years. My memories of him are touched with light and disappointment, flickering together in dark rooms among dusty books, with a fierce determination to beat the odds of circumstances and birth. His face comes to me in quiet moments, or at times I least expect, in classrooms and hallways among students and colleagues. The tears are always there, and they will stream forever. It is a welcome face, but a poignant one, a face I can never forget.

My house was small and the home comforts were few, but that didn't matter so much in the beginning. I cleared chicken feathers from the kitchen and chased armies of cockroaches around the bedroom by flashlight. I ate with Balingilaiki for the first week, stiff ugali porridge and thin meat stew, and baked in the evenings under the heat still radiating from my tin roof. I had known that the teaching might be hard, but I wasn't prepared for the poverty of resources at hand. Balingilaiki showed me the bookstore. He seemed embarrassed as he fumbled with the padlock. Inside the stifling room I could see why. Piles of old textbooks were strewn about the floor. Most were old grammar books written for British schools, dry and dusty and eaten through by termites. Apart from a few structure texts and some books of guided composition, there wasn't much I could use at all.

"The key is in the office," said Balingilaiki. "Come here any time. There are so many books."

On my first day in class I discovered that the blackboard was painted with gloss paint and was thus impervious to chalk of any kind. Chalk was our only visual aid, and so the boys rubbed sand into the board by hand to roughen the surface enough to hold a chalk mark. There was a spirit duplicator in the office, but the reservoir was dry and no spirit was available. The thick, black ink leaking from the Gestetner in the corner warned against attempts at use. It would be chalk and talk and whatever else I could turn up from the dark recesses of the bookstore.

Under the bulging ceilings, bowed by leaking rain and bat droppings, the classrooms were large and well-lit. Outside the windows, golden flowers swayed in the breeze. The flowers gave off a sticky resin which the boys used as glue to seal their letters home. In an attempt to stave off tribalism, boys were bused to boarding schools far from their tribal lands. Under Nyerere, primary education was universal, usually at soil-brick schools in the villages, where children learned to read and write together with a rudimentary English. Beyond this was a chasm. Only one child in a hundred had access to secondary education. The students at Bwiru Boys', ranging in age from 13 to their early 20's, were either well connected in party circles, or like John Samuel, clever and lucky. John Samuel sat in front, at the first of the rows of ancient wooden desks fixed to the classroom floor by iron staples. His concentration was intense and his brow perpetually furrowed. He wrestled the conundrums of grammar with a fierce concentration and asked question upon question with determined, polite insistence. His motivation was unwavering. It was new to me, this kind of passion for learning. It was unsettling too, in the burden of responsibility it carried. Success in education was life or death to John and his family, and my stick of chalk and limited experience seemed poor weapons to bear in the struggle. From the beginning, making a difference didn't seem like such a simple thing at all.

Africa beguiles and Africa shocks. There are no comfortable safety nets. Life and death are stark and clear and often they are not choices. On my visits to the town, the images of poverty never failed to move me. Beggars with outstretched hands, women selling bottles salvaged from garbage to hold medicines from the clinic, barefoot children under heavy loads, empty stores and cripples on street corners. The price of sisal was down on the world market and the price of oil was up. The Tanzanian economy was reeling, and all the fine words in political books and speeches couldn't alter the basic hardship of life. The atlases and textbooks had not prepared me for the truth. The point where ideals and reality diverge may be in the twisted limbs of a cripple who drags himself in the dust to beg, or in tears of loss shed in a dormitory by a schoolboy weeping quietly among lines of iron beds.

There was a 'Maktaba' at Bwiru Boys', a library, and for me it seemed a place of salvation. The building was shuttered and dark. Luogo said the boys stole the books to sell and so the library stood locked and unused at one end of the courtyard. I begged a key and poked among the dusty clutter inside. There were a dozen rows of shelves, mostly empty, but some lined with old encyclopedias and classic novels. There were manuals and books of nonfiction donated by the Ranfurly Library, culture-bound and useless. Along one wall, piled on the floor among the brown lines of termite tracks, were scores of hardbound copies of "On the Rural Socialist Question," densely packed propaganda shipped by Kim Il Sung from North Korea. None of it was much use to a reading teacher struggling without texts. But there, on the last row of shelves deep in an unlit corner, was treasure. Rows of simplified readers at all levels, classics of African literature by Ngugi and Achebe, the simple, luminous prose works of Nyrere—two hundred books altogether—a foundation, something to build on. Luogo agreed to open the library in the evenings but only on condition that I supervised and didn't allow the boys to carry the books away. I arranged some tables and chairs at one end, but the boys came in such droves that most had to sit crosslegged on the floor. John Samuel never missed a moment. He was waiting at the door at sunset every evening, brow in its perpetual furrow, eyes keen and eager, clutching to him the little red book he carried everywhere, his talisman, his dictionary.

There were no lights in the library, and on the equator, darkness fell at the same time each day. The boys strained to see in the last traces of afterglow before they lit the lamps. The lamps were made from old margarine cans cut and soldered into rough cone shapes. Kerosene provided fuel for their stuttering, sooty flames. In my mind now is the image of John Samuel, surrounded by the bowed heads of others, eyes glowing in the dim, flickering light, gazing at print. He questioned often and made prodigious lists of words to carry off and learn. I knew about acquisition, modern methods of vocabulary study, but there and then the lists seemed better than nothing and the only practical way. I sense them still as I write, the riffling pages of the dictionary, the dark shadows cast by oil lamps, and the luminous face of a boy intent on learning to the very depths of his soul.

The rains came and beat on the library roof. John Samuel shivered by the dictionary in the damp night air, cold under his thin white shirt as he studied. Classes were sporadic, and for three weeks now the boys had been digging in the fields to plant cotton for the school self-reliance project. The project was to raise money for school funds, to pay for books and equipment. Each day they dug, hoeing and raking at the red earth, preparing for the cotton seeds the government would send. They were not to know that the little blue seeds would be diseased and would not germinate, that all over the country the long rows of earth would lie barren and empty in the cold winter rains. It was at this time I recall, for I was duty master for a two-week stretch, that John came to me as I stood under the dripping trees in the courtyard. His head was bowed and his shoulders were heaving gently. As he approached I could see the tears coursing down his cheeks. He stood before me and stared at the ground.

"What's the matter, John Samuel? What has happened?"

He took a deep breath to compose himself, but when he spoke he could not hide the sobs.

"The dictionary," he said. "My dictionary. It is gone."

The Oxford English-Swahili Dictionary cost four hundred and fifty shillings in 1979. This was a month's wages to a town dweller, considerably more to a subsistence farmer from the countryside. For John's family to scrape together such a sum was an immense investment of faith and trust. I could only guess at the hardship and sacrifice it entailed. For his family, John's education was their one hope for security, money for old age, the certainty of food for his siblings. And the dictionary was gone, stolen while he worked, lost forever to the petty black market fueled by poverty and desperation.

"We will look for it," I said, though in truth I did not hope to find it. I assembled the boys in Sekou Toure dormitory and made them stand by their beds. Each boy laid out his possessions on his iron cot and stood to attention by his open locker. John Samuel, as a member of the dormitory, laid out his possessions too. Among the towels and cheap clothing, the exercise books and pencils, there was no dictionary. The boys glanced sympathetically towards John Samuel, but there were no clues, no information. At last I reached the rusting cot beside which John stood, quietly shaking. On the thin cotton mattress was a single, ragged shirt, a battered tin bowl and a toothbrush made from the splayed fibers of a green stick.

"Where are your other things?" I asked.

"These are my things," he said.

I looked again at the shirt, the bowl and the toothbrush, and tears welled in my eyes too. It was a moment before I could speak.

"We will keep looking, John Samuel. Perhaps we will find it. Perhaps you can get another."

And I looked at his face, the face that stays with me always, his eyes desolate now, clouded by loss and fear, the tears running down his satin cheeks and falling in silence to the dust below. It was a lie, I knew. Born of compassion, but a lie no less. The dictionary was gone. There would be no other.

John Samuel studied still. His grammar was flawless in our classroom tests, his determination unshakable, but his progress in reading and writing was slowed. In the library, his word lists were shorter. Without the dictionary he could only beg translations from my inadequate store of Swahili vocabulary. He stared for hours at the print, clinging to the hope that somehow he might find a matrix in the words. All around him the lamps flickered, their flames fragile in the cold air blowing in from the darkness of night. I wanted to help him more. I wanted to make a difference, but on a volunteer's salary I could not buy him another dictionary, and the circumstances of his life were beyond my power to influence. The realization came hard that the gulf between us was passable only by the flimsiest of bridges, chalk and talk and a few library books strewn over wooden tables, a brief word of welcome and a passing smile.

After two years my replacement arrived, Aisha, a Chagga from the foothills of Kilimanjaro. She was keen and realistic, ready to work hard for such small reward. John Samuel was beginning his final year, studying for the Cambridge certificate, hoping for a government job and a salary to send back home. I left on a warm evening in June, riding the green Bedford to the station down the red murram road, my mind already leaping across the miles to England. John Samuel was one of many boys who shook my hand and waved as the truck pulled off into the distance. Some of them would write, begging for books and assistance, but I never heard from John again. I hope he was successful. I hope his life became less painful as the years passed, but I do not know. I will never see beyond his face now, the face I can never forget. It is tempting to be sentimental, to say that I left a piece of myself in Mwanza, that I yearn to return, but I do not. I took away far more than I ever gave, and I carry it around with me as memories which surface in quiet moments of reflection, or when pink sunlight flickers on calm waters at sunrise, when I remember John Samuel, his spindly legs and his falling tears, and I wish him well.

Reaching the Target

Michael O'Laughlin, Lake Tahoe Community College

I sat on one side of a square formed by several tables, opposite two narrow windows that hardly shed light. Framed by brick walls, the room occupied one end of the fourth floor of the English-Philosophy Building on the Iowa River. The clock recorded the passing of 4:30 p.m. Since it was Tuesday, a hallowed hour had arrived. Famed for decades for turning out accomplished writers, this was the Iowa Writers' Workshop, and the room was Frank Conroy's.

Writing had been my habit for many years, but I could not have explained to anyone the essence of the act, or what lies beneath the drive to put words to paper. My personal experience with writing was for many years nothing more than self-expression, possibly because through taste and habit, I had been drawn to writers who were most like myself, writers with my passion, my loves, my obsessions. For ten to fifteen years of my adult life, the concept of reaching an alternative view had never occurred to me. To reach for the writers who did not easily or automatically touch me through the rhythm and tone of their first line was something I had not done.

Then I sat in the brick room for the first time, and Frank Conroy, the most memorable teacher of my writing life, took a small piece of chalk and formed the letters *W* and *R*, divided by a substantial space. Then he chalked an arc that rose like a missile from the letter *W* and ended it just beyond midpoint in its trajectory. At a spot below and farther to the right, where one might anticipate the missile sent by the *W* would fall, sat the reader's *R*. The writer, *W*, had sent an arc of energy *toward* the reader, but not all the way to full contact. The line of communication hung suspended in a theoretical space.

Frank then placed the chalk above the *R* and traced out another arcing missile, this one headed for contact with the writer's arc. The reader overshot the writer's point of completion in the space that divided reader from writer. The fact that the arcs do not intersect but instead overlap illustrates the potential for failure in each reader/writer contact event, but the diagram conveys the event, and the diagram seemed to illustrate the essence of what happens, or is supposed to happen, between reader and writer.

What is so effective about this diagram is that it so clearly illustrates the requirement of energy on the part of the reader. For students who have struggled with reading all their lives, it is something that makes sense to them. They are introduced to the fact that reading is a co-creative act, and that without their focused and concentrated energy, without their taking responsibility, contact with the writer will fail. This represents a new door for them, pointing in a new direction that they believe they might try taking, because it is something they have not been doing.

Two years later, I discovered as a teacher how quickly I had forgotten the essence of what I considered my most significant lesson.

At Lake Tahoe Community College, my developmental writing students are made up of several groups, represented substantially by middle-aged re-entry mothers, eighteen- to twenty-five-year-olds who had given up on high school years before, and ESL students who are ill prepared for the class two steps before the standard freshman English course, Reading and Composition. In the spring of 1995, I taught for the first time the lowest-level reading and writing courses the college offered. I discovered that these classes were the heap where anyone was thrown who did not qualify for the first-level analytical class that would prepare a student for freshman Reading and Composition 101. What this meant was that I experienced a spectrum of students who at one end needed nothing more than a review of grammar, all the way to the other end, made up of those with grade-school writing skills. But it was out of this group that came the student who became a prime lesson for me as a teacher.

Pete was a high-school dropout who always showed up for the evening class, but who after a month of classes still had not turned in a paper. He took all the vocabulary matching quizzes and other quizzes designed to smooth out grammatical problems, quizzes where the student had to either insert or take out commas and periods. One night, when we had read a story in which there were several student characters with dialogue, I asked for volunteers to read aloud, to act out what the story presented. Pete was the only person to volunteer, and he took the biggest part. He stumbled and crawled through the page-and-a-half passage, sounding out words aloud, while the rest of the class stared silently at their open texts.

"Thanks, Pete," I said when he was finished, grateful that his humiliation was over and that we could begin discussion.

For the next few sessions, I continued to have a hard time getting this group beyond monosyllabic responses to any reading, but the class energized at any aspect of learning presented as a game or that resulted in a numbered score that would not be graded, so I timed them with a passage that charted reading speed followed by questions on comprehension. When I saw that everyone was finished reading and Pete was still only halfway through the material, I went randomly among the desks, back and forth down rows, handing each student a piece of paper on which I had written his or her reading rate, hoping no one would notice Pete did not get one, thus sparing him the embarrassment of being so far behind everyone else. As I went on into the vocabulary-building phase, Pete kept reading.

Halfway through the vocabulary, Pete finished his reading and looked up. After a moment of my ignoring his signal, he said, "Don't I get one?" I quickly scrawled the figure on a piece of paper and gave it to him, 62 words per minute, compared to the average of nearly 200 for the rest of the class.

A week later, I decided that perhaps the slow response to discussion might be due to the students' failing to read the essays carefully enough in advance of class, so I told them we would begin writing very brief essay responses to the readings. The next afternoon, I started into the stack of quizzes in the college Learning Assistance Center. I had gone through most of their surface responses that illustrated little depth of understanding or analysis when I reached Pete's. A glance at the presentation was shocking. I thought of Dave, one of my colleagues, who had said just a few weeks before, "What I don't understand is the people here who just clearly don't belong here."

I had agreed but said nothing as another teacher said, "Everybody belongs here."

That response seemed to me like a political statement, because, clearly, not everybody belongs in any setting. But what the second teacher was saying was that for some people, there is simply no place else to go, and for them, the community college may represent their only chance at a new start. Yet when I saw Pete's scrawl across the page, I knew Dave was right. There were those who did not belong, and Pete was clearly one of them.

I tried to decipher Pete's first line, a blocky, shaky print style, tortured in its turns and looping of letters, done in a dull pencil, the lines wandering both down and up: "Beky thiks hur techur iss buyest."

It took a lab aide to inform me that the last word was 'biased.' The condition ran all the way through the quiz. I did not know what to do with him, and as was always my first reaction to discovering a student I knew I could do nothing for, I considered the most efficient way out, which was probably to tell him he could not pass the class and send him to the Learning Disabilities Lab for testing. I knew Pete wanted to be in the class, that his decision to return to school was a major one. He was a lift operator at the Kirkwood ski resort, and I had seen these workers swinging chairs in blowing snow for minimum wage. I had difficulty with the clash of his goal of rising to a life beyond that of a "liftie" and my desire to process him out of my class as quickly as I could. Knowing he would balk at dropping, it was a question of how quickly I could fail him.

I tossed the quiz aside. An *F*. He wasn't even close. Later that day, to bolster my decision to give up on him, I showed the quiz to several other teachers as they happened into the lab.

"This is unbelievable," ran the typical response.

Even the teacher who had said everyone belonged here shook his head at the level of the expression.

With such support, Pete was finished, as discarded as he had probably been all his life in educational programs and in workplaces and anywhere else he had been compared to others.

Then Dave came in, Dave who couldn't understand why those who clearly didn't belong here were here. And I handed the quiz to him, more as testament to his view than for any other reason, to say, "You were right."

I awaited his response. Dave had a Master's in linguistics, and after a moment, he asked to see the other quizzes. I gave him the small stack. He read them over. Dave had taught the text before and was familiar with the stories. Then he looked over Pete's again, the others' again, then back to me.

"He understands the story."

I forced myself to look again. I had been deadened by the vague, shallow quiz responses from the rest of the students who had remained on the surface of the material, giving no evidence that they understood the meaning behind the material. Than I swam slowly through Pete's tortured language, through his struggle to communicate with me. And indeed, perception was there, trapped behind the flawed print. Pete had understood the story, and it appeared that he was the only student who had. I had told the class that this quiz was not on grammatical precision, not to worry about it. I wouldn't take off for spelling or problems of sentence structure. I simply wanted to know that they had read the work, and how much of it they had comprehended. Now Pete's paper, based on comprehension, was suddenly the best in the class. And I saw my failure to allow him to reach me. I had failed in my responsibility as expressed by the diagram of the arc. Pete did not have the ability yet to cast his energy in words up to the point where my energy would reach him, because I had immediately turned off my energy when I saw his pencil scrawl, assuming there could be nothing behind it, nothing communicated, nothing perceived, nothing worthy. Pete sat there, the *W* in the formula opposite my *R*, unable to reach me because I had made no effort. I had somehow reverted, as a teacher, into that inert object I had been as an unsophisticated reader before being introduced at Iowa to Frank Conroy's arc.

I discovered at that moment that for all my great evaluations and for all my exceptional ability to teach creative writing, I was unsophisticated at what I viewed as the low end of the spectrum of a writing development teacher. Dave had exposed my flaw in a single moment.

As the quarter progressed, and I struggled along, I evolved into forming class-created paragraphs on the board. I gave the students the first line, and they had to logically create the second line, then the third, then the fourth. In this way, they seemed to begin to comprehend the mathematical analogy of writing, that each sentence presents an equation, and that that equation leads to the next sentence; that a sentence cannot be just anything; that it is dictated by the logic of the sentence before. But when the class would falter into silence, unable to move on, it was Pete's slower thinking process that came to my rescue, time and time again, with the next logical step. And of course, when he spoke, his words were not misspelled. And his suggestions were always a logical resolution into what could follow: the next thought.

Over coffee before class one evening, I told Pete that because of his lack of written work, I didn't see how he could pass the course. He was disappointed and promised me he would get his work in. But we were over halfway into the course now, and he still had not turned in an essay.

"Because you haven't turned in any work, I should have dropped you by now, but I do think you're getting something out of being in the classroom, so I don't want you to think of this experience as a failure, no matter what happens."

"I . . . I know I'm learning." Pete sipped his coffee, stared off into space. "I'm gonna try hard to get all that stuff in, but even if I have to take the class again, you're right, I'm learning something and that's the important thing." He said it in his slow way, and I knew that Pete would be with me either until the end of the quarter or until the final day of the option of Withdrawal. It would be an ironic "W," given what the "W" stood for in the arc and how Pete represented possibly one of the most significant "W's" in the arc that I had experienced as a learning teacher.

On the night of May 13 of a spring quarter in a winter that would not end, the students had read a short essay and we were going through the comprehension questions and the vocabulary matches together. Out of the sea of silence that the class gave back, something I seemed incapable of overcoming, Pete answered question after question, both the comprehension choices and the vocabulary ones. It almost became a show as Pete took his streak forward.

"An 'A' for you tonight, Pete. You got them all."

He beamed from beneath his beat-up baseball cap that read Echo Summit, a bankrupt ski resort, obscure even in its operating days. "All right," he came back. He grinned around the class. "Never thought I'd get an 'A' for anything. Least I can say I got it this one time."

It was a figure of speech for me, but I put it in the book.

Pulling out of the parking lot after class, a shadow flashed across the forest ahead, and I didn't even recognize it as a bicycle until it was past me. But I recognized the helmet I had seen on Pete's desk all quarter, and Pete abandoned the paved road and cut down through dense pines he could not possibly see, following a route he must have memorized in the way that some cannot read signs but know where to go by the physical landmarks of the world.

What Pete taught me is that there are no signposts in the road of teacher/student interactions on which one may depend. Minds must be open and reaching from both ends of the arc. What I thought Frank Conroy's arc had meant at Iowa was this: "You are an energy source and I am an energy source, but we stand on opposite sides of a sea of space. You cannot reach me unless I move toward you, and I cannot reach you unless you move toward me."

Frank was a powerful voice for me, and his voice is still with me, and I make certain these days not to enter any class, from the most advanced creative writing workshop down to the first developmental step, without the echo of his voice. He was my most memorable teacher, as Pete was my most memorable student, but what I also learned from Pete is that a refined interpretation of the arc is required, and I have come to think of this refinement as the "Covenant of the Arc": *You have an intelligence that I will acknowledge no matter what preconceived notion of you might stand in my way, and my search for the point at which our arcs meet is the Covenant of the Arc, my promise to you as your reader, and your teacher.*

Frank called it being grounded, turning something abstract into something concrete. And the concrete is what I preach as the foundation of writing.

Made for Each Other

Mary Sheehy Moe, Helena College of Technology

Renae has masses of mahogany-colored hair, three children, and an inordinate affection for chocolate. She once vowed that after high school, she would never again endure an English class, but here she is.

Cindy is afraid of school—and almost everything else. She sits in the back of the room, slumped forward over her table, a veil of fine brown hair covering haunted eyes. She doesn't want to be here.

Dale doesn't want to be anywhere. A year ago, he was an ironworker building a bridge in central Montana. It was Indian summer, and the branches of trees etched gold into a true blue sky. Dale remembers glorying in those etchings just before the truck hit him, pinning him to the guard rail and crushing his right leg. Now he's in my classroom because he has to be . . . to get the voc-rehab money. Besides, it doesn't really matter where he is. One place is as bad as another.

These are my students—never the carefree coeds of media mythology, sparkling with the kind of brightness assured by parents' money or confirmed by SAT scores. They're usually not teenagers, either, kids fresh out of high school, confident of seizing the world-their-oyster. Most of my students never believed the world was their oyster and don't believe it now. They are here for many reasons, noble and ignoble, but somewhere in the middle of most of them is a hope—faintly flickering, but there—the hope that this time school will make a difference. An associate degree in data processing, auto mechanics, or accounting will give them something to hang onto, a job, security, a future. That's what they want, and that's what Helena College of Technology is for.

The catch, of course, is that they have to take English—English, which they hate with a child's loathing of spinach. It may be good for you (they're not entirely convinced), but the very thought of it gags. And the minute they see me—or more precisely, the minute I open my mouth—their worst fears are confirmed. Listen to her, they think, with the proper grammar and the mile-a-minute delivery and the words, words, words! Their hearts sink. What are we *doing* here?

People like to think life makes sense. If life makes sense, you can manipulate destiny, make plans and decisions that will ensure a certain outcome. Maybe for some people life does make that kind of sense, and for them, explaining the decision to become a teacher is easy. They can connect attitude to action, or trace the effect to a series of causes, or perhaps show how one stunning event, some single, significant episode, was an epiphany for them. Like Paul struck by lightning on the road to Damascus, the message hit them: by George, I must teach!

I'm not one of those people. I can't make sense of life; I simply live it. For a long time, I pretended to myself that I made logical decisions, that the big events of my life—getting married, having children, becoming a teacher—were planned, deliberate acts. But in all honesty, it isn't so. In each case, it just felt right at the time. Now, *why* teaching felt right—that's the interesting question.

The first day of class is always the worst because on the first day I have to show the students the text we will be using: *Modern Business English*. It's thick, with small print and no pictures. Each chapter is cunningly named after a part of speech and filled with ponderous explanations and wearying worksheets.

This is not the way a course like mine should be done, I have been telling the administrators since I arrived. You can't teach language skills this way. It's demeaning, demoralizing—and futile. But the business department believes that these are the skills students need and bases later courses in the writing sequence on this approach, so I've been playing along and biding my time.

"This is the text for the course," I announce, holding up *Modern Business English* like a set of bad x-rays. As I summarize the contents, Cindy retreats further behind her hair and Dale looks out the window. Renae shifts in her seat and snorts: "English book from hell!"

We all laugh.

I should hate the institution of school because it betrayed me—twice. The first time it made me believe that succeeding in school mattered; the second time it fooled me into thinking that it didn't matter at all.

In grade school, I loved learning, especially English. I devoured the stories in the readers, stories with heroes, people with character who saved the day—or died in the effort. I was particularly taken with a series of "child biographies" of famous historical figures. They were all orange, I remember, and had the same sort of title: *George Washington, Boy Leader; Davy Crockett, Boy Pioneer; Benjamin Franklin, Boy Inventor.* Boy-oh-boy . . . the message was there, but I didn't get it. I truly believed that my gender difference was just a technicality; I, too, could be a hero, a winner. By dint of effort, my native gifts, and character, I could be anything I wanted to be.

Wasn't I already proving it? I was at the top of my class academically, the queen of the spelling bee, a leader on the playground. And—proof positive that I was a winner—I could play baseball.

Right from the start, I loved everything about it. I loved learning what a body could do—the beautiful rhythm of run-catch-throw with feet flying over grass and the glove an extension of the hand. I loved the thinking parts: figuring out where to go and where to throw, when to lead off and when to tag up, how to tighten up a hot box, how to round a bag. Above all, I loved the shock of *me*, a girl playing a boy's game: the skepticism when I took my stance in the batter's box, the big eyes when I cracked a sizzler down the third base line; the whoop when I nailed a throw from center field to the cut-off man.

"Wow! You sure don't throw like a girl!"

"I'm not a girl!" I would respond. "I'm a tomboy." Sweet denial.

High school threw my lie in my face, rubbed my nose into the real world of 1964, when the rules of the game for boys and girls really were different—and immutable. Girls were required to wear dresses; boys could wear whatever they wanted. Girls were required to take home economics; boys took shop. Athletic girls could play intramurals on Monday nights for diversion, but no team sports offered serious competition. Boys had football in the fall, basketball and wrestling in the winter, and track in the spring.

The coveted place of glory for a girl was on the sidelines, cheering on the boys amid the rustle of pom-poms, or keeping the crowd entertained at halftime with a Vaselined-permanent smile and a dazzling display of sequins and skin. The coveted place of glory for a boy was in the action itself, the main event. Under the lights of packed stadiums and gymnasiums, boys could stomp 'em, tromp'em—kill'em, by God—and somehow in the process build Character.

That was the crux of the difference. Boys had characters to build; girls had reputations to preserve. The very phrases sum up the tone of the times: boys had futures they could actively pursue; girls had pasts that they must passively preserve. Boys had choices to make that would shape their lives. Girls knew their lives would be shaped by being chosen.

In this world of homecoming queens, cheerleaders and majorettes, tomboys didn't get chosen for anything. I went from grade-school hot-shot to high-school pariah in one summer. The reading, the spelling bees, the beautiful world of sandlot baseball—all of grade school—had been a cruel hoax. None of it mattered at all.

We are studying pronouns now, in the early stages of our tour through the English book from hell. This book doesn't even pretend to be kind. Instead of easing students slowly, provocatively, into the intricacies of language, it intimidates. The pronoun chapter drones on about number, gender, and person for a page before presenting its usual far-fetched sample sentences, certain to daunt whoever survived the opening palaver. One of the sentences is this one: It is *I* who *am* grateful.

Dale snorts, "It is *I* who am grateful? Give me a break! Who talks this way, Mary?"

"You got me," I tell him.

"And am *I* grateful!" Renae chortles. "Why do we have to study this?"

At bottom, I tell them, insistence on the King's English is mostly just snobbery. People understand you perfectly if you say "It's me" instead of "It is I." In fact, seen from a certain light, "It's me" is preferable, since people get so tripped up by the surprise of "It is I" that they forget your message.

But it's like knowing which fork to use. If you get the food into your mouth without making a mess of yourself, you can use a salad fork, a dinner fork, a spatula or a shovel, for all I care. But the world is full of people who want to dismiss you for a technicality, and unfortunately, bigotry about language can do more than keep you from some snob's dinner table. Some people judge your ability to communicate entirely on the basis of your mastery of "the King's English," and they won't hire you, won't take you seriously, if you can't choose the right fork. Of course, what these people never seem to realize is that the fork they insist on using also keeps them from a lot of *our* tables. You can't say "It is I who am grateful" in Butte, Montana, and expect anyone to want to spend time with you!

Cindy has pulled back her hair for this spiel and at the mention of Butte, her eyes glitter. She spent her early childhood in Butte, a frontier mining town famous for its colorful people, stories and expressions.

"You're right," she says in a quavering voice. "Butte is a *very* exclusive society."

The rest of the class turns to catch a glimpse of this person in hiding, but Cindy veils herself once more.

No society was more exclusive than high school in 1964. The wrong hair style, the wrong shade of lipstick, a hemline an inch too long or too short—that's all it took to be the object of scorn. I could catch a line drive on the run in center field and throw the ball hard and straight enough to put a man out at third, but I couldn't get pink plastic rollers in my hair in anything approximating a neat row. My make-up looked like a mask. The way I walked and talked and sat revealed all too clearly that for me, heels and girdles and bras were instruments of torture.

The playing fields were gone. There was no recess in high school, and even a slow learner like me knew better than to try to join the boys in the sandlots after school. I had always had girl friends to play with before, but now the girls scorned play. All they did was gossip and giggle and feel their hair. For two years, I tried to find a niche, someplace where I could shine and be the star that I alone knew I was. There was no place for me.

Then I discovered parties. It was high school's answer to the American dream. Anybody from anywhere, regardless of hair, clothes, or gender, could be noticed. All she had to do to be accepted was "party hearty." To be admired, she could ride a motorcycle at breakneck speed down dusty Montana roads or drive a flat-tired car along the railroad tracks across a river. And at Montana's age-old teen institution, the beer kegger, there were always games: jumping over bonfires, tumbling down hills, running from cops. I didn't need algebra, English or biology. I didn't need cheerleading. I had found a way to win without sports. I was *in*, at last.

It doesn't take much time with the English book from hell to depress my students. Their earliest memories of feeling stupid begin to come back in waves—waves of nouns that look like verbs, prepositions that look like adverbs, and gerunds that look like participles. Too much time with the book thrusts them once again into that sea of words, words with labels but no meaning. They don't want to feel that way again, to drown helplessly under the unrelenting weight of the King's English. I don't blame them.

So we leave the book frequently to consider broader communication skills. Like how to interview for a job. It's real. It matters. It's why they're here. We focus on giving good answers to interview questions, how you can develop an answer with details, how you can organize those details through sequence, enumeration or narration. The students write out their answers and read them to each other.

This is how we learned what happened to Dale. The interview question was, "Tell me about a disappointment you've had." Dale wrote about the day he lost his leg, how he was mesmerized by those golden trees and saw the truck too late. He wrote about the months of recovery, his separation from his family, and his decision to go to school. "At first," he concluded, "I felt bitter about what happened to me. But coming back to school has been a good thing. I never thought of myself as much of a student, but learning about computers has made me realize that if I put my mind to something I can do it. In fact, I enjoy doing it. I think I'll be the same way on the job."

When Dale finished reading his answer, Renae of the Uncontrollable Impulses blurted, "Dale, baby, you are *beautiful*." We all laughed to put clothes on this naked sentiment, but when Dale looked around the room, he knew the truth. Something soft came into the flinty eyes. I knew just how he felt.

By the time I was a senior in high school, my reputation was established: I was wild. School was just a place to plan the next party. The achievements that might have been mine—Honor Society, scholarships— went to students who still believed that good grades made a difference. My report card was heavy with C's. I flunked chemistry—skipped it 44 out of 45 days one spring quarter so I could cruise with my first boyfriend in his '55 Chevy. It is amazing to me now that, of all the hours I spent in the classroom in high school, practically nothing emerges as a distinct, individual memory. I remember being ridiculed once as I walked down the row in my history class . . . my mother had cut my hair too short and my attempts to style it in a "pageboy" were a complete disaster. I remember a friend in geometry class slumping out of her desk and onto the floor like melted chocolate—we had skipped the pep assembly earlier to conduct some sort of drinking contest in the parking lot. And I remember the day Mr. Nesbit read my story out loud.

Somehow, I had managed to stay in the honors program in English, and Mr. Nesbit taught the senior section. One day, late in the year, he encouraged the class to do some writing for the school's literary magazine. A story began to take shape in my mind immediately, and I scribbled furiously through the rest of my classes. It was a true story about a time I lost my temper with my sister. I gave it to Mr. Nesbit the next day, and the day after that, he walked into class, sat down, pushed aside the day's lesson plan and read my story to the class.

I remember everything about that moment: how I folded my hands and looked down at the play of sunlight and shadow on my interlaced fingers as I listened to my words coming out of someone else's mouth. When it was over, the other students, most of them Honor Society members, looked at me as though they had never seen me before. And for the first time, I could look back at them with pride, not defiance.

More and more, I push the book aside and contrive assignments that give students the chance to tell their stories. We call it "being out of the book." Renae tells us about chocolate and her children. Bruce writes about his car wreck; Chauntelle, about her music. Their stories make them come alive and give them dignity. Because they want to tell them well, they consider their words carefully . . . which happens to be the objective of the course.

Cindy tells what she can. There is a fire in her big story and someone dies in it—her daughter, I think. Her little stories are sad ones, too. In December, Cindy approaches me after class, shaking as always.

"I might have to miss sometimes this month, Mary," she says in her quavery voice. "Christmas is hard for me."

"I'm sorry, Cindy. Come when you can."

Cindy pulls her hair back, revealing the frightened eyes. "You remind me of my mother, you know," she says, half-smiling.

"Really? Well, thank you!" I reply.

"It's not a compliment." She sees my startled look and adds, "But I like *you,* Mary . . . when we're 'out of the book.'" She laughs and the hair flops back down.

I didn't decide to become a teacher when Mr. Nesbit read my story to the class. I never made that decision. I went on to college and chose English as a major because I had always been "good at English" and figured it would be easy. Nothing I experienced in college changed my mind about the importance of education; after all, I would be getting married, having kids, raising a family. It didn't really matter. Then the world changed again and it turned out that it really did matter after all. Married or not, I needed to work. My degree was in English, and the job you get with that degree is a teaching job. So I teach.

Sometimes I wonder what I might have been if I had stayed on course. But I suspect that I was on course all along, that perhaps I was destined to go back to school as a teacher and get it right, *make* it right.

In twenty years of teaching, I've had many different kinds of students in many different settings. For years, I taught advanced placement English to those sparkling ones, the high school kids who go on to Harvard, Stanford, MIT. That was fun, too. But Dale and Renae and Cindy need me more and seem to know me better. They understand about losing things and getting lost. It's like we all went to the same high school—or maybe we're just made for each other. At any rate, sometimes I feel like a hero in this job, someone with character who is saving the day. More often, I feel like I'm surrounded by heroes. Either way, it's a pretty good way to feel.

Teaching Atop an Eyeful Tower
Ethel Tiersky, Harry S. Truman College

Inside Room 2426 at Truman College, I've worked with students from Argentina to Zaire and every letter of the alphabet in between. The world has walked through my doorway and enriched my life immeasurably. I've taught my students English and a bit of American history and culture. But how much more have they taught me! From their conversation and writings, I've learned how *kimchee* is prepared, what's inside the Hermitage in St. Petersburg, when the rainy season comes in Vietnam, how a Buddhist monk lives, and a thousand more fascinating facts. As I've struggled to teach them English, I've received an education in linguistics. But information is just the tip of the iceberg. My ESL students have taught me the most important things I needed to know—how to teach, how to relate to others, and how to live.

Teachers often share tales about foolish mistakes their students make. But my students make mostly intelligent, logical errors. When English breaks its own rules and tricks them, I sometimes get as annoyed as the students. After all, why shouldn't the opposite of *sunshine* be *moonshine*? And if we can say *he isn't*, then why not *I amn't*?

Occasionally, my students' errors are downright inspiring. When asked to write a composition about the most interesting place he's ever visited, Vladimir described his visit to Paris, where he journeyed to the top of the "*Eyeful* Tower." Reading his essay in my office, I laughed 'til I cried. Then I realized that I'd never noticed that *Eiffel* and *eyeful* were homonyms. Finally, my mind played with his serendipitous spelling error. A metaphor led to an insight. College professors are often accused of living in an ivory tower. But not I. My ESL classroom, I realized, was an eyeful tower. Sitting atop my classroom desk, I have a unique world-wide perspective. And the view is breathtaking!

The longer I teach ESL, the more I marvel that *any* non-native speaker is able to learn English. First of all, English has the largest vocabulary of any language. (*The Oxford English Dictionary* lists about 500,000 words, and there are another half-million technical and scientific words.) To make matters worse, a single word often has many meanings. (The record number belongs to *set*, which, says *The Guinness Book of World Records*, has 58 noun uses, 126 verb uses, and 10 uses as a participial adjective.) Then, too, the speaker of English often has a choice of several words to express basically the same idea. In addition, students must deal with figurative meanings. One of my students, who worked for an architect, approached me with this puzzling story: "My boss said my drawing was too busy. How can a drawing be *busy*?"

Native speakers don't even notice, but English has literally thousands of phrasal verbs that are grammatically tricky to use and extremely easy to misunderstand. For example, *give up* has nothing to do with *giving* anything or with moving *up*. Pity the poor foreigner, having to memorize the meanings of *take up, take on, take off, take out,* and *take in.* The single phrasal verb *make up* has about fifteen meanings, and several more if you add *to.* The British often turn their noses up at American English in which, they say, one can communicate virtually any action by using a phrasal verb beginning with *get.* (Try it. It almost works.) The ESL classroom has taught me to appreciate the difficulties that face non-native speakers and to be tolerant of their mistakes.

My students have also pointed out that my clearly enunciated, formal English doesn't prepare them for what they hear in the street or on the job. They ask for definitions of *gonna, hafta,* and *wanna.* Questions such as "Whachadoin'?" or "Whereyagoin'?" leave them quite mystified. I've learned to teach colloquial English along with academic English. In fact, to adequately prepare them for the real world, it's a good idea to teach the meaning of *ain't,* even though, in my classroom, they ain't allowed to use it.

All my students wrestle industriously with this impossible language, knowing that they must get it under their control. The foreign students need English in order to complete college (and perhaps also graduate studies in the U.S.A.) so that they can return home with the skills and credentials their countries need. The immigrants know that a decent future depends upon achieving a fairly high level of English. Most of them have lived intimately with hardship and some with terror. Thus far, their new lives in the U.S.A. have given them little except hope. Once they were doctors, engineers, factory supervisors, and school superintendents. Now, they return to the classroom as students. That isn't easy. But they do it with their self-respect intact. They maintain a zest for life despite the roller-coaster ride it's given them. They present a more inspiring lesson for me than I could ever create for them.

Serious is not the opposite of humorous. My students have taught me that (to paraphrase Mary Poppins) a spoonful of humor can make the lesson go down. Laughter and learning blend together very nicely, thank you. Mistakes? They're expected. They, too, add spice to classroom life. My students have taught me to be comfortable with imperfection, theirs and mine. Together, we laugh and learn from truly wonderful errors such as these:

"My ankle came from out of town."

"I usually get a seat on the bus, but this morning, I got a stood."

"For breakfast this morning, I ate my mother and father."

Though their sentences are sometimes funny, I tell them (truthfully) that they're doing infinitely better than I. Although I studied four different languages during my school years, I can't converse in any of them. I've lost what limited foreign language skills I once had. Disuse leads to disappearance. In fact, except for my ongoing struggle to master computerese, I haven't developed any major new skill in years. I'm impressed by these people—some middle-aged (as I am) and some elderly—who are still playing the learning game. They remind me that an exciting life requires mental growth. I'm ashamed of my stagnation and vow to do better.

My students want to understand not only the English language but American culture as well. However, much of what they see in Chicago's inner city astonishes and frightens them. With weak grammar and strong emotions, they express their horror as they view the worst of American life. Alcoholics lying in the streets, the elderly lying in nursing homes, children lying to their elders, dope addiction, crime, the death of God, the birth of illegitimate babies—they notice and decry it all. Yet, though they get an eyeful of the worst of America, they continue to respect its best. Freedom, democracy, opportunity—abstractions all, but palpably concrete to them. The openness of American society gives them a sense of optimism and a feeling that, here, their destiny is within their control. Boris expressed the views of many when he wrote, "In general, I like America in spite of now I have a lot of problems, but I believe that everything depends on me." Everything depends on me. What a powerful and empowering thought! Boris taught me that I'm important because I can make a difference.

Summarizing a reading about the Westward Movement, Irene's eyes filled with tears. She was embarrassed. I was overwhelmed. The thought of a government that actually helped people, that gave them dreams instead of nightmares, was enough to make her cry. The Westward Movement will never seem quite the same to me again.

No matter how convoluted the grammatical path gets, my students are determined to follow my train of thought. If I haven't been clear, they let me know. When, midway into the lesson, a student moans, "I'm getting a headache," I give myself an F, back up, and try a different approach. I can count on my students to tell me when my words come tumbling out too fast, my explanation is muddy, my exercises are too difficult or too boring. They've taught me to present only one principle at a time and to review, review, review. In short, with patience, and a multitude of tactful suggestions, my students have taught me how to teach.

That's not all. My students have also taught me to see beyond the group of language learners and view them as individuals with personal lives and careers. They notice my new dress and my new hairdo. They ask about my vacation plans and my children. By example, they've taught me to relate to them in personal ways. Thus, we have real conversations. While we practice English structures, we share our lives. Eventually, we become friends working together toward a common goal.

Respect, my students have taught me, must come full circle. "Why don't they know that?" I used to wonder. "I taught it yesterday." Was I once curt when the same question came at me twice in the same lesson? Probably. But now I know that it may take seven repetitions before my knowledge becomes theirs. Still, as long as they come to class, listen, and try, they deserve my respect. I owe it to them because they treat me respectfully.

Sometimes I get it right, and my students give me the greatest gift of all—they learn what I'm trying to teach. As their English improves, they give me more credit than I deserve. After all, I'm not the only one teaching them English. Their other teachers are classmates, neighbors, coworkers, store clerks, TV set, car radio, and so on. Living in an English-speaking country, the language surrounds them. They can't help but learn more of it. Nevertheless, they give me the credit for every English word they know. So I get the beautiful flowers at the end of the semester.

If not flowers, then food. Maria, a 35-ish plump, motherly student, arrived at my office door with one plate of home-baked cookies and two little boys. She was going to drop her sons off at home and then go to work, she told me. "Where do you work?" I asked, just making conversation.

"At the whore house," she replied cheerfully.

"Context. Consider the context," I reminded myself. I'd been teaching ESL long enough to know that all communication must be considered in context. I *had to be* misunderstanding her. "*Where* do you work?" I asked again.

"At the whore house," she repeated. I must have looked pained because she added, "You know. It's on Belmont and Broadway." I sank back in my chair, much relieved. Yes, I knew it well. On Belmont and Broadway, there was a branch of Jane Addams' famous *Hull* House.

The homemade cookies were delicious. But I've received more memorable gifts. One of the nicest was delivered on my 57th birthday. That morning, my mirror reminded me that I was approaching my "golden years." My laugh lines were no longer a laughing matter. Nevertheless, during the grammar lesson that day, Israel made me feel like Miss America. Demonstrating his mastery of the adjective clause, he completed my sentence, "The woman who . . . " by saying, "The woman who is our teacher is very pretty." These days, some would call that sexual harassment. But coming from a 64-year old student to his 57-year old teacher—well, it made my day.

For the past twenty years, I've been teaching ESL full-time. My classroom experiences have permeated and enriched my entire life. When I leave the classroom, wherever I go, I am especially tuned into the nuances of English.

Eight years ago, I was lying in a hospital bed awaiting diagnostic surgery to determine the cause of my sudden hemorrhaging. My anesthesiologist dropped in to explain his role in the surgical procedure. He was a calm, pleasant gentleman with a Vietnamese name sewn on his hospital cloak. "We must to do this," he said almost apologetically. "You know, we have to stop your breathing." Those terrifying words almost stopped my heart. Then I remembered. It was a natural error for someone from the Far East. The age-old confusion of *l* and *r*. My friendly anesthesiologist only wanted to stop my *bleeding!*

Diagnostic surgery was followed by curative surgery. A few nights later, I found myself in the care of a young nurse named Ingrid, another immigrant. I was in pain, but it wasn't quite time for another shot. "Do you want talk for a while?" Ingrid asked me. "It will maybe to help you forget pain."

"No," I replied. "I'm too weak to talk. You talk. Tell me how you learned to speak English." So Ingrid talked, shared the story of her youth, distracting me until I fell asleep. The next morning, an American nurse came in to check on me. "Ingrid was here last night," I told her.

"Oh, dear," she said. "Could she understand you? Her English is so terrible."

"On the contrary," I corrected her. "Her English is wonderful. It got me through the night." The primary goal is communication, not perfection. My ESL students taught me that. I hope I've taught them as much.

Hidden Harvest

Linda Boynton, Oakland Community College

I didn't know what to think when I first saw it. I walked into my office, the last day before Christmas break, lugging two bookbags full of writing portfolios. On my desk was a small assortment of Christmas gifts given to me by students the last few days—homemade cookies, a couple of tree ornaments, and some stationery. But this morning I found on my chair a large grocery bag full of potatoes and a little green Christmas card tucked into it. Puzzled, I opened the card and skimmed to the end to see the giver's name. It was from Theresa, a student in my developmental writing class. I picked up one of the potatoes and brushed away a few clumps of Huron County dirt caught between two bumps. Then I picked up the heavy bag, still cellar cold, and ran my hand over the smooth wrinkles that come only from folding and refolding. I placed the bag on my desk and thought about the young woman who had surreptitiously placed it there.

Theresa was a 26-year-old mother of four who had just finished her first semester at Jordan College, a small two-year business school located in an economically depressed rural part of Michigan. Jobs were, and still are, scarce, especially for young, unmarried, uneducated mothers. For example, one discount department store that opened in the area announced that it had received 5,000 applications for just over 100 positions.

And so they came to Jordan—laid-off factory workers, unskilled high-school graduates, and many, many young women who had "bought the line," believing the words of some young man who promised home, children, and picket fences. These women grabbed onto these airy promises, sacrificing educational goals to get the lives they *thought* their mothers had. Theresa was one such young woman for whom it had all fallen apart.

Theresa was always quiet in class, listening and looking at me intently, at least until each time we made eye contact; then she would avert her eyes. One day, almost halfway through the term, the assignment was to write about something you do well. We were reading some of the papers aloud in class, and I asked Theresa if she would like to read hers. She looked down and said she didn't have her paper ready for today, which surprised me because she was always very prepared. After class she came up to me and handed me her paper, explaining, "I just didn't want to read aloud. This is about the only thing I know how to do. And it ain't much that anyone would want to hear about."

I looked at the title: "Growing Potatoes." Then I sat down and said, "I'd love to hear about growing potatoes. Tell me."

And so she did. She brushed the hair out of her eyes and sat erect. She looked me straight in the eye and explained how to grow potatoes. She even smiled, showing slightly neglected teeth, as she talked about the first time she won a ribbon for her potatoes at the county fair. And now, on that day before Christmas break, fresh with the promise of the season, I looked at this unusual Christmas gift and certain words she said floated back to me.

Potatoes grow underground. You can't really see what you've got unless you take the trouble to dig it up.

That's what it's like teaching in a community college. Each semester begins with a sense of excitement that is tempered by apprehension because I know much of what I have to work with remains buried. Ryan's love for poetry is buried under his contempt for teachers. Karen's strength to defend her ideas in an essay lies buried under years of abuse, first from her father and then from her husband. Darin's ability to finish something he starts remains buried under years of enthusiastic beginnings that all fizzled into failure because of an indifferent family. And Theresa? This young mother with four children, who spent six days a week working in a laundry, washing and ironing the clothes of other people—what had she buried? Like many others, she had lost her ability to dream, to imagine a place where she and her children could not simply survive, but flourish. This was starkly pointed out to me in the first writing assignment I gave that term—to write about what the perfect world would look like. With her caring yet relentlessly beaten view of the world, she wished that there would be enough homeless shelters for homeless people—she didn't wish for enough homes, only enough shelters. There was much to be cultivated.

There are a thousand varieties of potatoes. You didn't know that, did you? I can tell.

No, Theresa, I didn't know that, I thought as I looked at this gift she had left. A thousand varieties, just like our students. No matter how much we try to classify them, they each come to us with their own hybrid histories. No one knows that better than those of us who teach developmental writing. These students, trusting us, place their memories on paper the way rust appears on an old car—slowly at first, not at all pretty to look at. We give them some tools, and they begin to scratch away the corrosion, often revealing pain underneath. It can't be predicted or prevented. It just *is*. And no two stories are the same.

Some crops are better than others, but you learn a lot from all kinds. Growing things wouldn't be much of a challenge if you always knew exactly what you were gettin'.

Such is the nature of most developmental students' first attempts at writing. Some of Theresa's work was hurried or done without careful thought—for a variety of good reasons—and I had to resist the temptation to give her a higher grade or accept less-than-quality work in order to make her "feel good." I know from experience that we give students a lasting sense of self-esteem only by giving them the skills to excel when they leave us, not simply to feel good about trying while they are *with* us.

And so Theresa did the rewrites. I gave her praise for each change, and like most students who had been little noticed in their lives, I could see her filing away my comments, so she could bring them to mind again and again, the way a shy teenage boy remembers each word a popular girl absently utters to him in passing. And her skills became stronger and stronger, at first hinting at, and then ultimately mirroring, that special drive that kept her going.

We give some of the potatoes away. People cut them into pieces that include eyes and replant them. Then they grow again somewhere else.

These are the secret rewards of teaching in a community college. The effects of what we do often remain hidden from us. Yes, we sometimes hear what happens after our students leave us. In the mail I've received first "real" paycheck stubs with smiley faces drawn on them and invitations to graduations from four-year colleges. One developmental student even went on to be nominated for a Michigan Press Award. But mostly the healthy roots spread in silent ways that we never hear about. Parents become positive role models for their children or other family members. Cycles of failure get broken. Students, once content with low-paying, unfulfilling jobs, begin to want more, which means they find the courage to face rejection instead of letting it control them. And eventually things begin to happen.

Some of those seeds grew in my own family. Recently I was helping my son pack as he began his own college years. On his dresser I found a shriveled-up, lightweight piece of something black and started to throw it away. He stopped me with a brisk "No!"

"Why? What is this?" I asked him.

He took it carefully from me and said, "It's just something I keep to remind me about, you know, important stuff."

I then realized it was one of the potatoes from that bag. I had brought it home that evening, three years ago, and my husband, son, and daughter at first laughed. I told them the story of the gift, and we all became quiet for a moment. My daughter had tears in her eyes, and I remember my son taking one of the potatoes out of the bag. *People cut them into pieces and they grow somewhere else.* Yes, Theresa, you're so right.

I am now studying for my Ph.D., not because I want a raise or want to teach at a four-year college—neither of those things would be true even with the degree. I am studying mostly because I find I'm a better teacher when I'm also a student. But the other Ph.D. candidates who take their English studies "seriously" perplex me. They see teaching in a community college as a last-ditch option if no tenure-track positions open up. In a course I just finished, we read several diverse texts dealing with oppressed populations. During discussions, the other students would lament their inability to help, wanting to leave their present positions to join the Peace Corps or VISTA so they could do something that *really* matters. They are looking for dew-kissed peaches and plums and pears—shining, sweet, visible validation for their efforts—certainly not potatoes.

It frustrates me to think they need to leave where they are to make a difference. Why do we not understand that as teachers, we are witnesses to and responsible for a social miracle in our classrooms every day? Circumstance brings together, for a prescribed period of time in a controlled, academically "open" atmosphere, diverse segments of the population who would *never* otherwise congregate. After teaching for twenty years, I have become more and more aware of the enormity of this responsibility. But I suppose that if you are teaching subjects and not substance, if your students accumulate points instead of points of view, if after they leave, you judge how much *you* have given *them* instead of how much *they* have given *you*, then perhaps I can understand why some dedicated teachers scurry to find some socially noble (and highly visible) outlet for their guilt. But I am saddened by this.

I would like to tell you where Theresa is now, but I don't know. She has moved on and so have I. Now I teach at Oakland Community College, a two-year school that serves almost 30,000 students, but Theresa sits in each new class I teach, gently reminding me that unharvested food rots and withers away. I can still remember the words on the card she left with that bag of potatoes. She wrote, "Thank you for giving me the gift of language. I found my voice and the courage to share what I have *right now* instead of waiting to share the things I hope to someday have. These are all I have. So far. Love, Theresa."

If only we all were so rich.

The Right Teacher at the Right Time

Nancy Carriuolo, University of New Haven

Crash, my blue and white parakeet, strutted nimbly across the top edge of the library book I was reading. Occasionally, he leaned down to peck at the pages, trying to lure my eyes back to him. I pursed my lips and blew gently on his face to shoo him away. I had to concentrate. After all, I was allowed to read for only thirty minutes each day. My demanding little feathered friend had all the rest of my time and attention.

As an eight-year-old confined to bed for the winter and spring, my world was as small as the one captured in my favorite Christmas present, a little glass dome filled with imitation snow and a scene of a family singing carols. My doctor came daily to give me shots of penicillin, and my teacher came every Friday after school to give me assignments; but they were the only outside visitors to my family's fifty-acre farm in upstate New York. In 1956, my rheumatic fever (and its look-alike cousin, polio) frightened people away to a safe distance.

As much as I dreaded seeing the doctor, I looked forward to seeing my second-grade teacher, Mrs. Marian Schultz. She swept into my tiny bedroom looking tall and imposing in her Lucille Ball-style full-skirted dresses with wide belts. She carried a brown paper bag, in which she had everything she needed to teach. Every minute counted, so she used to dump the bag onto the foot of my white chenille bedspread as soon as she arrived. Sharpened pencils, a couple of library books, handmade get-well cards, and what looked to me like a small mountain of mimeographed assignments rolled, spilled and drifted out of the bag. As she picked through the items, she chatted with me, deftly reconnecting me to her classroom.

"Nancy, all the children send their warmest wishes. Becky, Linda and John were all out sick this week with bad colds. The other children made some cards for you. Oh, look at this one. Crash is pictured on the cover. He looks a bit more like a buzzard than a parakeet, but I'm sure that's him," she chuckled, holding the hand-drawn card up near my face.

Mrs. Schultz always took a few moments to make known the presence of my phantom classmates before we started my lesson. She reported their illnesses, their difficulties with particular assignments, and their magnificent moments, such as the time my best friend Betty massacred the boys during a game of dodgeball.

Of course, chatting lasted only long enough to recreate the atmosphere of our classroom. What the chatting ended, her laser-beam questioning began: "I brought you more library books. Are you finished reading *The Borrowers* yet? What did you like about the book? What didn't you like? Unless you express your thoughts very specifically, Nancy, I can't select the best books for you." As her only pupil, I never needed to raise my hand. Mrs. Schultz kept firing variations of the same question until I managed to return an acceptable answer.

At the age of eight, I was learning to be specific not only in my evaluation of literature but also in my choice of language. Mrs. Schultz softly corrected my grammar and pronunciation in a way that made me mindful of linguistic choices without making me ashamed of my background.

Leaning forward in her chair so that her brown eyes were directly above my blue ones, she said matter-of-factly, "There's nothing wrong with the way your family speaks, but I want you to learn a more formal kind of language to use in school. You speak differently with children than with adults, right? Well, in school I want you to speak and write yet another kind of language, the same kind you read in your books and you hear me speak. OK?"

While Mrs. Schultz stoked up my mental powers, Crash usually cruised the room, deciding whether to execute a dramatic crash landing onto Mrs. Schultz's shoulder or onto her head. He was particularly partial to her reddish-brown pageboy because I always laughed at the sight of him perched on the top of her head with his tail draped rakishly off to one side like an outlandish decoration on a designer hat. After several lessons, my mother tried to banish Crash to his rarely-used cage in the dining room, but he shrieked until I began to sob, so Mrs. Schultz decreed he could stay for our lessons as long as my attention was focused on her, not him.

Surely, Mrs. Schultz must have felt confident she could easily squelch the antics of my spoiled parakeet. She was the first teacher I had ever seen calm a roomful of crazed children without raising her voice. Sometimes she just stopped speaking and stared. Other times she placed her hand solidly on the shoulder of the group's ringleader. She was friendly without being motherly, and my classmates and I were never too sure what she might do if pushed too far. Discipline was never much of an issue for Mrs. Schultz.

One of Mrs. Schultz's greater challenges was to teach me cursive writing. My doctor did not allow me to sit upright in bed unless necessary, and he did not consider writing to be a necessary part of my recuperation. Since I had to lie down, clearly my writing paper had to be held upright. My mother quickly grew tired of holding my writing pad, and Mrs. Schultz found the task even more tedious. During the second week of my writing instruction, Mrs. Schultz suddenly asked my mother to call my father out of the barn and into our kitchen. She had decided to have my father craft a wooden prop that would angle and secure the paper for me. My mother and I exchanged nervous glances. My father, a taciturn, no-nonsense Germanic patriarch, was not used to being either commanded or instructed, especially by a woman. From my bedroom, I listened intently for what I assumed would be, at best, a stalemate between two very strong-willed people. My teacher briefly explained to my father the height and angle needed and the purpose of the proposed writing prop, but then she asked his opinion of the best material to use and listened with seeming interest while he talked about carpentry and the cabinets he had made for our kitchen. As Mrs. Schultz deftly guided the conversation, I heard my father beginning to embrace the project as his own contribution to my education. As a child, my father had dropped out of school after sixth grade in order to help support his family. He didn't appear interested in either my school work or my mother's efforts to tutor me. Through Mrs. Schultz's eyes, though, I began to see that, perhaps, he simply needed a way to participate. My father picked out the wood for my writing prop, drew a rough plan, and wielded the saw and hammer with pride and enthusiasm. Everyone, including Mrs. Schultz, seemed to forget that the original idea was hers.

Even Crash eventually became Mrs. Schultz's ally. In imitation of Mrs. Schultz, he learned to chant "Good, very good" like a mini-Greek chorus whenever I used my writing prop. Mrs. Schultz was a handsome woman with a Lauren Bacall voice that Crash never perfected, although he spent—perhaps to Mrs. Schultz's relief—more and more time listening to her and mumbling facsimiles of her favorite phrases instead of trying to use her as his unwilling straight man. Crash worked on his linguistics while I worked interminably on my writing.

Years later, teachers complained that I held my pen like a club, and the resulting writing was less than elegant. Considering the tenacity required for those particular lessons, their description of my approach to writing was (and still is) probably accurate. Writing from a prone position is not comfortable, and the Palmer method of drawing endless circles and practice letters is dreadfully dull. I can understand why some students never become adept handwriters. However, Mrs. Schultz was determined that graceful or not, I would learn to write. Periodically, she reminded me that in order to complete second grade, I needed to pass a final examination that included demonstration of my ability to write. *Ergo*, she stated emphatically and repeatedly, I would learn to write. Just to keep the goal in sight, sometimes she talked about Miss Burke, the third-grade teacher, and all my nearly-third-grade friends. Mrs. Schultz held the bar while I made mental leaps.

Near the end of my lesson, Mrs. Schultz always called my mother in from the kitchen, which was adjacent to my bedroom. We reviewed what I had learned and what I needed to practice in preparation for the coming Friday. My mother, who dropped out of school after the ninth grade, was an enthusiastic teacher's aide. Between lessons, she relentlessly recited Mrs. Schultz's endless mental math problems and spelling quizzes while she stirred stews and soups simmering on top of our combination wood/coal stove. I suspect now that some of the assignments were not given to my classmates. After all, how likely is it that the second grade memorized the state birds of all forty-eight states? Crash's periodic deviltry probably sparked that particular assignment. Anyway, while my muscular, tomboyish body withered, my mind strengthened.

By 4:30 p.m. every Friday, I could hear the motor on Mrs. Schultz's 1954 Ford revving up as she raced home to feed her own husband and daughter. I had thought that women quit work when they got married, but Mrs. Schultz showed me a different possibility. At the end of each lesson, she politely expressed regret about leaving me, but she also spoke enthusiastically about going home to her family. Sometimes she described what she planned to make for dinner. I wondered if she had two brown bags, one with my work and another with their dinner. Along the ten-mile route from the primary school to my farmhouse, there was a country store that stocked one or two cans and bottles of everything from bag balm to sardines, as well as a few fresh items such as breads and cakes. I pictured her handing Mr. Chilson, the proprietor, a neatly printed alphabetized list of grocery items to gather and then strolling the narrow aisles of his store, picking out a chocolate cake or fresh rye bread. I was certain Mrs. Schultz had money for such luxuries; after all, she was a teacher, and surely teachers must earn as much as doctors (or so I thought until I received my own first teaching contract).

By the very end of the school year, I was able to walk a few steps to the window in my bedroom to watch a robin who had built a nest on my window sill. After the speckled blue eggs hatched, Mrs. Schultz discussed the chicks' feedings and their later flight instruction, presumably as my weekly science lesson. The mother robin was very accommodating. She seemed to sense that we were safely caged inside my bedroom, so she went about her mothering and teaching chores with little attention wasted on us.

Mrs. Schultz was particularly interested in the chicks' flight lessons. Years later the mother bird's teaching strategies became my mnemonic for recalling the principles for successfully teaching developmental students.

"Look, Nancy, see how she takes her tiny, weak chick out for extra short flights while the other baby waits. He needs to strengthen his wings before he can keep up with his lessons," Mrs. Schultz whispered, half to me and half to herself. (We weren't sure how to tell the sex of the baby robin, but we conspiratorially decided the smaller, weaker bird was a male.)

Without using educational jargon, Mrs. Schultz explained to me many of the facets of good teaching as we watched the smaller of the two baby birds struggle to keep up with his sibling. On one particular day, an especially fierce Canadian wind blew over my house from nearby Lake Ontario. Facing into the wind, the tiny baby could barely stay upright on the telephone wire, where his mother had left him while she escorted her other baby to a nearby cherry tree.

"See how she flies ahead showing the way, but then circles back behind, chirping and urging the chick toward her goal?" Mrs. Schultz remarked admiringly.

Suddenly the wind was too much for the little bird left clinging to the telephone wire. He swung around nearly in a circle. The mother bird headed back to him, chirping what we imagined to be "Hang on! Just hang on that wire!" By the time she returned, he was upright again, but clearly terrified. She perched next to him and chirped comfortingly at him, but then she began to urge him out into the wind with her. Usually, she brought the stronger chick back to the wire before setting out with the weaker chick. This time, though, she must have decided that he needed to brave the wind immediately before another sharp gust blew away the remnants of his confidence.

"She will take him to the maple tree. It's closer than the cherry tree. She wants to give him a taste of success. Then they will rest and move on to the cherry tree," Mrs. Schultz predicted.

Of course, she was right. Short-term, achievable goals; positive reinforcement; frequent practice and feedback; and expert and peer modeling were strategies that Mrs. Schultz and the mother robin knew instinctively. I, on the other hand, was not as gifted. I never understood the power of these simple teaching strategies until the mid-1960's when Dr. Stewart Dube, my professor of Psychology 101, gave them labels and discussed them as part of our study of learning processes. Dr. Dube encouraged the class to develop personal mnemonics, and in the middle of his lecture, I realized that the robins provided me with a rich memory device. I could reconstruct the principles of teaching/learning by recalling the flight lessons of the robins and Mrs. Schultz's commentary. Even later, in the mid-1980's when I was President of the National Association for Developmental Education, my speeches before professional groups often began or ended with the robin's flight lessons as an analogy for effective developmental instruction; but I never acknowledged that my favorite analogy really belonged to my second-grade teacher or that I had been her developmental student.

Small incidents, such as the raising of a family of robins, were indelibly etched on my memory because my days were so barren. Periodically, whenever I was feeling especially sorry for myself, my mother perversely insisted that I was very lucky. After all, Mrs. Schultz was teaching me at home. Teddy, the classmate from whom I had caught rheumatic fever, didn't have weekly lessons. He was going to repeat second grade. I always wondered why Teddy didn't continue his studies. His mother was a nurse, and he was hospitalized. I knew that children were not allowed to visit, so it seemed logical to me that teachers might be excluded too. Whatever the reason, I decided that my mother was right: I was lucky, more lucky than I realized at the time.

My mother also frequently reminded me that Mrs. Schultz had fought fiercely for my right to study at home. Mrs. Schultz spoke with the school principal immediately after she conceived her plan to teach me while I recuperated. The principal was very reluctant, almost adamant. He felt that any youngster who missed more than six months of school clearly had not spent the state-required number of hours in class. Undaunted, Mrs. Schultz coached my parents (especially my mother) about my outstanding standardized test scores and my precocious promise and dispatched them to do battle with the principal and the school board on my behalf. Long before parental advocacy was a watchword, Mrs. Schultz used the concept like a crowbar to loosen a school system that was intent on counting hours of classroom instruction as proof of educational quality.

I realize now that Mrs. Schultz was not paid for teaching me after school hours. She often referred to herself as a volunteer, but my family never realized what she meant. My parents and I thought she was doing what she was supposed to do: teach. I never returned to see her after I began third grade in a new school near my former primary school. I never told her that Crash looked for her long after my lessons stopped, or that he died the next winter from a bad case of pneumonia that my mother and I naively tried to cure with steam from the teakettle. I never let her know that if I had repeated second grade, I might have carried on a family tradition of dropping out of high school. I certainly would not have become a teacher and later a tenured full professor. Without her example, I would never have guessed that each day contains enough time for a woman to raise a family and teach classes, as well as a little extra time for students who need and deserve more than traditional classroom instruction provides.

Mrs. Schultz was the most important of all my teachers because she came at a crucial time. Without her attention in primary school, I would have been labeled a failure and warehoused in classes with other students of and for whom our educational system holds no expectations. Mrs. Schultz's early intervention ensured that I was numbered among the so-called gifted when the launching of Sputnik began the space race and propelled all the most promising students into selective classes with special teachers. In my sophomore and junior years of high school, Mrs. Smith and Mr. Lubes immersed me in British and American literature; and in my senior year, aged Mrs. Butler (who claimed to know Julius Caesar personally) convinced me that the roots of all fine literature were to be found in the Latin and Greek classics. She also convinced me that I should become a teacher and arranged for me to teach her own Latin classes whenever she was absent. All three teachers encouraged me to apply for college scholarships. After I arrived at college, Oxford-educated Dr. Marchant taught me how to write like an academic and nudged me on toward graduate school, where Dr. Odell in his Texas drawl affirmed that a Ph.D. was within my grasp.

Clearly a chain of teachers and professors pulled me up the educational ladder, but without Mrs. Schultz's early intervention, I would never have met any of the others who came after her. In 1956, the country doctor and his bagful of needles and penicillin may have redeemed my body, but Mrs. Schultz with her bagful of books and papers redeemed my mind and my spirit.

Journal of a Gatekeeper

Elisabeth Bass, Camden County College

It's two o'clock in the morning. I've finished marking my Camden reading class's first departmental exam and except for too few, they did horribly.

I have felt so right in this classroom surrounded by adult learners, as I am an adult learner; urban public school products, as I am an urban public school product; and yet . . . These are voices we haven't heard speak for themselves. I teach these black and Latino/a adult students reading and writing because I want to hear their voices; I want everybody to hear their voices. But the rules are plain. In the state of New Jersey no one can take a college-level course without passing the New Jersey College Basic Skills Test—the NJCBST threshold competency examination, and I am the gatekeeper. If they cannot pass the departmental examinations, they are not even afforded the chance to take the NJCBST. I try, but half the class flunked this first exam.

Was it me? Was it the test? Was it them?

WHAT WENT WRONG?

Was it me?

I admit one teaching error—I should have taught the author's purpose as the defining marker of the rhetorical strategy. I taught Orwell's "Hanging" as narration, *"look for verbs, characters, plot—a story,"* but the test answer key specified that when an author's purpose is political, the strategy is argumentation—no room for discussion on multiple-guess tests. Who am I to argue? *(I'm new here, low woman on the totem pole. A new chant for me— teach to the test, teach to the test.)*

I could have assigned more homework *(most couldn't have done more)*. I could have given more quizzes *(there's so little class time as is)*. I could have/I should have/I . . . am a naive little engine that doesn't recognize the weight of the train she is trying to pull.

And then there's the test.

That test confirms my students' worst fears about reading classes—all those abstractions. A whole conceptual vocabulary of reading that is so easy to test *(and so meaningless)*. Does it help them read better before or after it drives them away from college?

"If you do not pass these courses, you cannot go on. I'm sorry."

I did not go into teaching to be a gatekeeper.

I should have created my own test. I should have stood up to the administration and created my own reading list too. (Damn, the publishing and legal world now keeps me from doing that. I can pull together more exciting, relevant readings, but I can't get them duplicated.)

Which means—I'm a rat *(for confirming their fears)* and a coward *(if I teach to an arbitrary test)*. And teaching has become labyrinthine.

Of course, there's always the students.

It would be easy to blame the students *(and so they don't blame me)*. I could give them a different kind of quiz:

(1) Whose fault is it if you flunk a test?
  • How many times did you review each article?
  • Did you take good reading notes?
  • Did you take good class notes?
  • Did you create a special study group?
  • How many hours have you devoted to this course over the last five weeks?

(2) If you have a less than competent teacher you should . . .
  (a) do nothing but quietly endure.
  (b) complain loudly and often.
  (c) flunk out.
  (d) study harder with friends and tutors.

I could walk in tomorrow and berate them for failing the exam. They are used to it. Most will take it well; some will not. No difference. It will be easy to point out how they failed; their guilt is always handy. No, they didn't study enough; no, they didn't really get into the reading about the man in India; no, their attendance is not that good; they're too tired in class; they're often unprepared.

See—being a gatekeeper is easy (all one needs is to be arrogant and emotionally dead).

But . . .

I did not go into teaching to be a gatekeeper.

I went into Basic Skills teaching to become a great teacher, a better teacher than I'd ever had in the Philadelphia public schools. Yet, even as a composite of the best I've experienced, I'd fail these students.

Fail these students. . . .

These students' motivations are the most compelling I've ever heard. They are in my classroom trying to escape death. This is not drama; this is Camden. For some, the alternative to college (and then a job) is King's "suffocation in an airtight cage of poverty." It's drugs and alcohol to numb the pain of watching their family and friends fall sick, get shot, hustle, lie, play the systems, fall prey to the systems, die often and early.

These students are the strong ones, but that just makes their burdens outside of class more crushing. As C. said to me, "Am I going to say no to my mother who bore me, now a tiny frail wisp of a woman; no, to a brother who is ill and can tell no one but me because it's AIDS; no, to my children— I am their only safety in this scary world!" *"No, C. you can't say no, but Latinas, you, the world needs you, with your degree, please C., stay . . . no, no. . . ."*

That leaves the system.

I become the No sayer; I become the gatekeeper, just another representative of the systems that say no to them: the welfare worker, the boss, the bill collector, the landlord, the . . .

doctor at Auschwitz, "You pass, to the right. You fail, to the left."

Back to the beginning.

Why am I here?

I became a teacher because I wanted to say YES: "Good, great! You're getting it! This is wonderful! You did it! I am so proud of you."

I will start again again. I will re-learn how to teach. I will demand smaller classes and do more with every moment. I can use the old ditto machine for new readings. We can ditto class notes, the students and I, and share the struggle. I will get the rights to copy new materials; I will learn how to do this. I will remember what I have learned.

Mina Shaughnessy begins her famous text on teaching with an image— she is sitting before a stack of student papers that she cannot respond to. Her students' words, their lives, their ways have given her pause. She understood that we must find new ways to respond that don't blame the students, that don't blame ourselves, that help to transform the system.

I did not go into teaching to become a gatekeeper.

And the students?

These students are motivated. They walk Camden's streets with their books like shields enscribed with "Loners survive." Attending school is a precarious balancing act that wrings the last bit of energy one has to sit by a light at night and try to study. Their motivation slaps them, accuses them of what they aren't every day of their lives.

But their motivation does not automatically mean extra time and attention to their work. By now they can recite books on study skills, what they **should** be doing. They've taken the special classes, workshops, created their own special survival skills. Yet I demand for them, for myself, that learning should not require the sacrifice of one's children or life. If only the most selfish, the most ambitious, survive, we will never hear the voices we need to listen to.

One study guide glibly remarks, "Rich or poor, you get 168 hours a week." But how many hours does one own as an individual? A working-class family and community survives collectively or it doesn't survive. And my students are the strong ones. So am I in the classroom promoting an individualism to save the few that can be absorbed into the failing economy, and fail those who refuse to "go it alone"?

I ask my students. Are you trying to become a nurse to escape your family, your community? Not the minority adult student. They recognize their debt to parents, spouse, kids, community more so than the middle-class college students I've taught. And they are probably correct in saying that if they aren't there ("yesterday, last week, last night, next week") to physically, financially, emotionally support this one or that one, then no one else will be.

These students are part of the only safety net that Camden has. They stood guard, in abandoned houses, against arsonists who would make Mischief Night the conflagration of Camden; these students have taken in this child or that one; they have gathered food, knocked on doors looking for pregnant teenagers, listened to the voiceless, cried, and prayed together.

I did not become a teacher to keep them out.

That leaves the system.

I could walk into that classroom and dump my guilt feelings on their backs and leave empty. Flunk 'em and forget 'em.

"You, to the left."

A few passed—the best, only the best. We must maintain standards or we fail them as well. Our brand of excellence or none. "You, to the right."

Or, I could curve the hell out of that exam, leave them thinking it's easier than it is, and a semester later, fail them. Then they would have to repeat the class, and finally, they would quit out of frustration, confirmed in their belief that they are too stupid to go to college.

"You, to the left."

Or?

I learn from this disaster. Teach more to the tests (while I try to change the tests). Ditto (while I try to change the course). Ask them to learn from this experience (while I try to change too).

Before I returned the tests, we sat in a circle and I read from my journal. The silence was awesome. I let myself tear before them. For a moment, a teachable moment, there was a tear in the cotton wool. Teachers are both gatekeepers and allies. Systems can be affected—there are real people in them. Minority adult voices are crucially important, but degrees (and true literacy) help to confer power. (And I can still curve the hell out of this one test!)

Dear Allise

Susan D. Bungard, Walla Walla College

Dear Allise,

I think you had been signing your letters "Love, Allise" for years before I could bring myself to make the transition between "Dear Mrs. G." and "Dear Allise." Addressing you by your first name seemed to defy the deep respect and admiration I had for you as a teacher. Now I realize that it was just that respect, almost awe, that turned an average high school English class into a room full of ravenous students: eager to learn from you, eager to please you, eager to do their best for you. You set goals—attainable, but challenging goals. Good grades were not within easy reach; we had to climb, to stretch, and always extend our abilities to the limit to reach them. And when we got there, it felt good. It really felt good. It made you feel good too.

We could tell when you felt good by the sparkle in your brown eyes. They danced. They really did. Your eyes would dart around the room, taking us all in, feeling our success, and your eyes would dance behind your dark-rimmed glasses. Sometimes you would chuckle, too. Even then, I knew you loved to teach. You loved to see us learn. And we did.

What did we learn? You taught us how to read like explorers, using our minds like tools; whether they were bulldozers, or spades, we were all in it together; digging, searching, experiencing language and literature in worlds long ago. You taught us how to write like artists, using words to sketch, sculpt, or paint our personal portrayals of the world as we saw and felt it. We learned to love words in your classroom. Words became our friends, our companions. We learned to respect words and use them carefully, judiciously. We learned to love words and use them playfully, joyously. I think we learned most of all that learning can be fun.

Learning was fun in your class because your energy and enthusiasm virtually filled the room. It didn't matter if we were diagramming sentences or reading Shakespeare; you seemed electric with excitement when you stood in front of the classroom. I sat in the front row, and you know what? I got CHARGED! Otherwise shy and unsure of myself, in your classroom I had a barracuda-like belief in myself. I believed I could accomplish great things with the English language. I believed I could beat out Craig or Sonja for the top "A." I believed I could be "somebody" someday. I believed, somehow I knew, I would carry what I learned in that classroom with me for the rest of my life. So far, I have.

At the time, I never dreamed I would carry what you taught me into my own classroom. I had planned to be a writer-slash-homemaker, or a home-maker-slash-writer; but single-parenthood forced me into the classroom in 1990, and there I stood—in frightened awe of those twenty-five pairs of eyes. This teacher thing, this wasn't me; what was I doing here? I was sup-posed to be at home, hunched over my word processor, drinking my morning mocha, and overhearing my son singing along with Mr. Rogers in the other room. But there I stood, and although I didn't think of you at that moment, something magical happened. I became electric. Just like you. I felt a surge of pure enthusiasm for being there, for having the awesome opportunity to share the spirit of language, and learning, and living with those twenty-five students. That's the way you felt, wasn't it? I think I carried that spirit of teaching with me for many years before, like a dove from a magician's cape, it fluttered out unexpectedly; and it surprised me most of all.

A few weeks ago I dreamed that I saw you at my twenty-year high school reunion. It was at a large cement convention center, which seemed like a giant gray maze. I wandered about, looking for my class of 1975, searching from section to section of the massive structure, going up and down steps, and feeling quite lost. Then I saw you. You were walking slowly, stooped, and using a cane. I called you and ran up to you. Your brown eyes danced. We hugged. "Where are they?" I asked. Of course you knew, and told me how to get there. But several flights of steps lay ahead of us. I looked at you, seemingly half of the physical person I had remembered you being, and I bent over and picked you up. You didn't protest. You laid your left arm around my shoulder; your shoes rested against my left thigh. I car-ried you up the steps, around the building, and into the reunion. Then I woke up. "Yes," I thought to myself sleepily, "I am carrying her. I am carrying her every day into my classroom." And I fell back to sleep.

Of course I can't really imagine picking you up, because I still remem-ber you as a five-foot-six-inch frame packed solid with sheer power. Yours was the kind of power that comes from a deep, utterly secure sense of identity that no one can really threaten. But that's using 1990's lingo. Back in the 1970's it was just, "Watch out for Mrs. G., man. She's tough. You don't want to get into it with her. No way." You welcomed challenge, though. You loved it. At the beginning of each year's class you announced that if anyone at any time heard you make a grammatical error, he or she would be awarded five bonus points. Five points! So we all sat smugly in our seats thinking, "Yeah.

I'll catch her. I'll do it. I'll get those five points." There were many attempts throughout the year, but you could almost invariably prove you were right. That was the thing. We knew you were right. You were willing to admit when you were wrong, but it just didn't seem to happen.

Yet underneath all of that toughness was a tenderness that ran just as deep. I knew you loved us all—from Brian who sat in the back row whittling his pencil with his pocketknife, to Andrea who sat front and center, never even brushing the back of her seat. You cared about us at that moment in our lives, and you cared about our futures. You seemed to have a vision of what we could do, what we could be, long before we did. Remember when we studied poetry, and you told me I ought to try to publish my poem? I believed in your confidence in me, so I sent it in to a magazine. Then, two weeks before graduation, I got the acceptance letter and the check. I felt like Hemingway himself. That wouldn't have happened without you. Somehow, back in those days of mini-skirts and Elton John, Watergate and Vietnam, you reached a roomful of restless teenagers and gave us the stuff to help build solid futures. Your toughness tempered with tenderness made you a teacher with incredible influence. I know it worked on me.

Even now, I think of you when I write. Although it has been nineteen years since you last graded my English papers, I still write letters to you as if they will be sent back, marked and graded. "Let's see," I ponder, "is there a comma there, or not? Darn. I should know." So I send a letter almost shyly, knowing you might find an error or two, knowing you will notice my handwriting becoming increasingly sloppy; knowing you will notice and smile, but disregard my imperfections. In a sense, I guess I will always be your student, and you, always my teacher.

Now many years have passed since you last stood in front of a classroom. Do I think of you, peacefully rocking in a rocking chair, your legs covered with a pastel shawl, as you read your favorite books? Not a chance! Now your "classroom" has become a retirement center! Your ongoing game of "Jeopardy" is a big hit among the residents, I've heard. I can just see you, busily passing out papers, probing, quizzing, gathering up responses, correcting, rewarding, whisking information from room to room, as your brown eyes dance all the while. It doesn't matter that your "students" may graduate to hospitals instead of colleges; you are helping them learn, helping them grow—still. Isn't that what teachers are for? You know, if there were an award for "Teacher of the Century," you'd be it. You'd be it, Mrs. G.

With love always,
Susan

Self-Judgment: A Student Discovers the Value of the Personal Essay

Michael Charney, Sussex County Community College

When Jennifer slipped into my Developmental Writing course that first night, she hadn't read a book in over sixteen years. The last one might have been something assigned in high school—perhaps *The Scarlet Letter* or *The Great Gatsby*. She couldn't remember. Whichever, it hadn't been memorable. Though she wandered through the educational system, nothing she had ever written, no completed assignment, had come from her own hands; she scrambled through with the aid of *Cliff's Notes* and misguided friends.

Not long after, her drinking grew steadily heavier, and she began using drugs—cocaine and heroin, mostly. But eventually—and in each life who can tell what event changes people?—she became aware of her own entanglements and began to unravel the strings of her own life.

She entered community college after a mere eleven months of recovery, an alcoholic and addict in her early thirties, shakily taking one day at a time, handling each stress as it if were uniquely hers. The first thin wrinkles had begun to appear at the corners of her eyes. The decision to re-enter school must have been a difficult one for her, coming as it had after so many desolate years.

My Developmental Writing classes begin with my students offering brief introductions. I do this because many arrive filled with an unjustified stigma: that a need for Developmental course work indicates something "wrong" with them, some personal failure. So I let them talk about themselves, and I offer an occasional question designed to probe, to remind each one of some event in their lives that has demonstrated success. My goal is to remind them that they *have* succeeded in the past—and I offer them the opportunity to reawaken that feeling, to believe that they can succeed again. But when Jennifer introduced herself, she started by telling us her faults—outlining what she could not do. "I'm too much of a perfectionist," she told the group. "And if I can't do something perfectly, I give up." As it turned out, she gave up a lot.

On the first night of class we give our students a brief diagnostic test, its purpose to make sure that the students are properly placed. Part of this test is a twenty-minute essay on a given topic. Jennifer's attempt showed six different opening sentences, each changed by only three or four words from the one above it, each a complete grammatically correct thought, and each crossed out so thoroughly as to be nearly unreadable.

We started on a freewriting that very first evening, taking several time-outs over the course of the three-hour session for some head-clearing scribbles. I walked around the room watching—but not too closely—each of them try to keep a pen or pencil moving, to let the stream of words emerge randomly, without regard to meaning or composition. They would work for a moment or two, stop, stretch cramped fingers (unused to concentrated writing), and then start again on my mark. Most of the students worked quickly and easily once they had down the basic concept, but Jennifer just couldn't shut her brain down; every word that leaked from her pen needed thought, careful choice. I sent her home with an assignment: "freewrite" into a tape recorder. Just babble. Let loose a stream of consciousness.

She found it difficult, but worked at it. I then suggested she transcribe what she had said into her journal—I have all of my students keep diary-like journals during the semester—but told her not to stop the tape while she was writing. If she couldn't keep up, she was just to skip a few words and pick up again with the voice on the tape—her voice. This technique, I suggested, would give her no time to think about what she was writing, and certainly wouldn't allow her the time for editing.

The technique helped; in later freewriting sessions she occasionally stumbled into detailed thoughts, but, for the most part, words streamed from her pen with nearly the ease they had into the recorder.

We moved into prewriting, learning how to cluster ideas and develop essay topics, and from there into brief but complete essays. Yet still none of Jennifer's writing assignments were any less abortive than her initial diagnostic essay; none approached completeness. A paragraph on how her parents met stumbled and drifted and, like a boat left tied to a dock, bobbed without direction. Another, about a Fourth of July picnic, blew up like a cherry bomb in her hands. These and others were commonly peppered with crossed-out words, restarted sentences, re-chosen ideas. It wasn't that she had difficulty with prewriting. She—along with the rest of the class—was building detailed clusters, random webs of information, and drawing from them numerous essay options. Jennifer's topics were tightly defined; her own opinions woven neatly into the pattern. But once she faced the empty lines of a notebook page she froze, only eventually working her way through a stuttering, correction-laden first draft.

I took her aside after class one evening. The hallway was noisy with the shuffling of students leaving classrooms; the sounds of teachers gathering books and rearranging chairs filtered through open doorways. "I'm not getting this," she told me, and I asked her what she meant by "this." "This writing stuff," was her answer. "It's not what I expected."

"It's not the writing," I told her. "It's me." She looked at me strangely, not sure of what I meant, but anxious to tell me that I was doing a fine job. I waved her comments aside. "What I mean is that you're too worried about what I think. What a teacher thinks isn't important. We all have different standards, for one thing, and, for another, we're only temporary. You need to write for you."

She nodded, agreeing, and told me that was exactly what she and her therapist had been working on. "I don't like being judged," she said.

This fear of judgment is common to Developmental students; in each class I teach nearly every student asks what it is *I* want. They ask about length, about content, about form, about grammar. They want to know how I *judge* them. It's a difficult habit for them to break, trained as they are for years at learning what their teachers expect from them; but I answer none of these questions. They need, I tell them, to work toward their own maximums, not to my minimums. "You're the only one judging you," I told Jennifer. "I'm an advisor here, someone to help you rebuild the fundamentals that you've forgotten over the past years, or were never even taught. And part of my job is to shake you loose from the idea that you have to please some teacher. I'm convinced that that is what's frustrating you. You *know* all this stuff. I've seen your journal. You have your own voice, things you want to say. You worry too much that I won't want to hear them, so you struggled to find some artificial voice that you think I'll approve of. That's all it is, really. You freeze up when you think you're being judged."

We parted; it was halfway through the semester.

The following week my students turned in the first draft of their major semester project: a personal narrative essay. In it, Jennifer had begun breaking through her barriers. Taking to heart my comments about writing for herself, she had gathered notes freewritten in her journal and had assembled a discordant tale of a life gone askew, describing in detail her journey into drugs and alcohol, her initial attempt at recovery, and her subsequent failures: "When my therapist suggested I enter a rehabilitation center," she wrote, "I fired her. It wasn't long after that I returned to drugs."

I again met with her after class, this time to discuss the process she went through in composing so moving a piece. "It's writing I've been doing for a long time," she told me. "For myself, as part of my recovery. I thought it was too personal. Teachers have always wanted stuff that was appropriate." I asked her what she meant by the word "appropriate," but she couldn't answer me. Again, I told her, it came down to judgment, and whose was more important, hers or mine.

Jennifer's first draft was far from complete. She had skirted around details, the examples often were not relevant, and her essay lacked organization and a unifying theme. I asked her what it was about. "My problem with drugs and alcohol," she told me. I reminded her that she wasn't writing a book, only an essay, and that she needed to be able to define, in one sentence, a single, detailed, central concept.

I watched her lips thin out and her eyes turn into camera lenses, watching me as if she were no longer participating in the conversation. Her grip tightened on the pages in her hand, and I could feel her frustration. I knew exactly what she was thinking: I was the one who told her that she should break through her frustration by writing for herself, by worrying not about being judged, but about what she thought. Now I was telling her exactly the opposite, recommending that she refine and edit, according to my advice. It's a point I believe all Developmental teachers reach: once you break through to your students, convince them that what you, the teacher, think is not the most important thing, you must then make the transition to having your students shape their own works into something cohesive, readable, and meaningful.

It was this last point I concentrated on. I asked Jennifer what her own paper meant to her.

She wasn't sure.

"Then why write it?"

I saw her start toward the obvious answer like a sprinter heading from the blocks. She wanted to tell me that she wrote it because it was an assignment, because her teacher told her, because she *had* to. I saw her realize, nearly as quickly, that the response wouldn't carry.

This was her real turning point: that it wasn't enough to write for herself as a writer, she had to write for herself as a reader, too; what Jennifer developed as an essay must mean something; otherwise the words were no more valuable than the aborted starts and stops that had marked her earliest, perfection-sensitive attempts.

Weeks later, her final draft: tight and driven with emotion, it earned her my highest praise. She thanked me, then told me she didn't need it.

"I knew it was good when I finished it," she said.

Of course, that was only in her judgment.

Teddy

Angela Maloy, Muskegon Community College

High-school freshmen accustomed to tidy packages of grade-school nuns were often shocked to see Sister Theodora. Grey hair squirted from her starched headdress. A row of safety pins dangled off the woolen folds over her large bosom. Keys collected since her first days at Saint Augustine Academy for Girls in Lakewood, Ohio, chimed against her wide frame, and large grey pleats opened and closed, opened and closed as she moved down corridors. If she hadn't become a nun, she would have made a good Hollywood bag lady. If those grade-school teachers maneuvered like efficient sparrows, Sister Theodora was an over-fleshed ostrich.

We began our work together in 1963. She was launching her thirty-fifth year at Saint Augustine's; I held a new and nervous bachelor's degree from Alverno College. She taught English to the high school's freshmen; I was assigned sophomores for American Literature and Latin II. Sister Theodora would act as my mentor.

Teaching has never sat lightly on my shoulders. Even now, after my own thirty years, I cannot sleep until tomorrow's classes are planned. Imagine, then, my jitters the day before the first *real* assignment. I wanted to memorize answers for every question students could ask. I felt inadequate, missed the intellectual safety of life as a college student, regretted not choosing instead to manage a fast-growing pizza franchise.

That afternoon Sister Theodora stopped into my classroom, where I was preparing for opening day by alternately pinning blue letters onto a bulletin board and crying. She took me outside for a walk.

"What if all the students hate me?" I asked between sniffles.

"They won't," she answered, reaching elbow deep into her grey pockets for peanuts, fodder she apparently stockpiled to share with friendly campus squirrels and hysterical first-year teachers. She listened as though my concerns were unique.

"What if they just refuse to do the assignments?" My nightmares featured groups of teenagers rising out of desks like plaid-jumpered devils and shouting, "No! You can't make us!"

But she assured me: "They're more afraid of you than you are of them."

After days of preparing study guides for *The Scarlet Letter* and devising ways to make participles interesting, I longed to be as relaxed as she, to crochet a scarf in the lunchroom or weed around the school rosebushes that first week of September. I had spent almost ten hours preparing my first day's lessons. How would I find time to plan day two?

"Just ask them a few questions, and you'll find out they didn't pay attention to you on Tuesday," she said. "So on Wednesday you do it all again."

Sister Theodora had become a legend at Saint Augustine's, and it was my privilege to work with her for three years. The association became, for me, a seminar in classroom management and educational psychology.

Every September, fourteen-year-olds with their hands over their mouths entered Sister Theodora's classes whispering and giggling. In June they emerged talking about Julius Caesar and paragraph unity. Every autumn they slumped and cracked gum. By spring they looked Sister Theodora in the eyes, distinguished metaphor from Mephistopheles, and never thought to mention that pins were falling from her black veil.

She sat behind her desk, overflowing the chair and holding a wide brown box of index cards, each headlined with the name of a student. During class she rummaged, pulled out cards, and called on girls whose names she had already memorized, whose mothers and older sisters she had eased through braces and boyfriends and Browning. She didn't try to entertain—no artificial jokes or contrived audio-visuals. She didn't care whether they liked her; she would like them. The girls responded to her honesty, as large as her body. While they did *Warriner's Handbook* daily, she'd admonish them: "You need to know this. Just wait until you get that sophomore teacher. She's tough." (This with a straight face as I stood, knees quivering, in the adjacent room.)

Sister Theodora's favorite squirrels were the mangy ones. She sucked noises between her widely spaced teeth, and they scurried to eat from her hand. She worked especially hard on the frailest rosebush, which by late summer blushed a bouquet for the school chapel. She thought that fat, awkward freshman girls needed extra cultivating too. For them she reserved special responsibilities. At Saint Augustine's the homeliest freshmen corrected spelling quizzes authoritatively, delivered notes to the principal, and proudly decorated hallway boards.

"I look into those eyes and see, ah, wilderness," she told me once. I watched and learned as she worked, little by little, to fill in the blanks.

In those days nuns usually kept to themselves except for professional concerns. I knew nothing of Sister Theodora's personal history. She might have been born in long black stockings and sturdy leather oxfords. She certainly seemed to know firsthand how awkward teens and insecure fledgling teachers felt. She did at times receive money from some relative, which she used to build a cache of prizes for freshmen successful in answering the brown box. In her special bottom drawer, photos of the Beatles mingled with Necco Wafers and tiny blue medals for wrist watches.

Funny, but I never thought of Sister Theodora as a holy person, even though she had lived vows of personal poverty, chastity, and obedience for almost forty years. We called her "Teddy" behind her back, and she knew it. She was more a large stuffed friend, more a Hallmark grandmother than a holy card virgin. Nuns were not allowed to attend weddings then, but many alumnae returned to Saint Augustine's on their wedding day to get Sister Theodora's approval of both their gowns and their grooms. Later, when they brought their infants to meet her, the babies chewed and drooled on her wooden rosary beads.

An article written for teachers offered this thought: "You will find out years later that students have forgotten much of what you tried to teach them, but they have always remembered *you*." I return to both that sentence and memories of Saint Augustine's when I need help keeping a balance in teaching, especially when it comes to developmental classes. Content is important, I know, but though she died years ago, Sister Theodora reminds me that there are *many* blanks to fill in.

Thousands of Saint Augustine alumnae are out there serving as nurses, engineers, homemakers, lawyers, mothers, and, yes, managers of fast-growing pizza franchises. They may lapse and split infinitives. They may even, sometimes, say "ain't." But I know that neither they nor I will forget Teddy and the many doors she opened without using her jangling keys.

How I Learned to Teach

Rita Smilkstein, North Seattle Community College

Twenty-five years ago I thought a student in my humanities survey course at the State University of Michigan was laughable when he wanted me to give him a date I had just said no one knows. He sat with his pen poised over his notes, looking up at me anxiously. "Just so you can fill in the blank in your notes?" I asked. "Yes," he said, not seeming to hear—or passively enduring—my sarcasm. "Oh, well," I said, "then write in 1676. It's not the real date, but you just go ahead and write it in so you can fill up that blank." He did.

I had an understanding of and loved English literature, my area of specialization; and I was good at lecturing on it. I was well organized, well prepared, and worked hard. However, I see now that I was not only not a good teacher; I was a bad teacher.

The next year, because of my husband's increasing illness, our family had to leave Michigan and move to New York near the hospital that had previously treated him. The only teaching job I could find on short notice was as a one-year replacement English teacher at a public high school. At this school I learned the first of three life-changing lessons that taught me how to teach. This lesson gave me not only my first insight into what teaching really is, but it also broke my heart because, not knowing enough to carry what I was learning through to the end, it broke some students' hearts.

One of my classes in this high school was a ninth-grade English class for students the school had identified as losers. There were eighteen boys, all minority and working class. Only two were freshmen; the others were 15 to 17 and couldn't be said to be in any grade. They were in their classes as in holding tanks until they were 18 and could be called seniors and would be allowed to graduate.

After two weeks with them, I felt I would not be able to go on. They wouldn't listen, they wouldn't work, they wouldn't stay in their seats, they wouldn't stop being disrespectful to me or to each other. That fifty minutes a day with them was so agonizing that after two weeks I wanted to quit my job. But I couldn't quit; my husband was in the hospital and I had to support our family. Instead, I thought if I could identify the major conflict between these students and me, perhaps I could resolve it. I came to the conclusion that I wanted to teach and they didn't want to learn. This conflict could be resolved only if I stopped wanting and trying to make them learn.

The next day I came to class with a pile of automotive and sports magazines and said to them, "I figured out that the problem is that I want to teach but you don't want to learn. So you don't have to learn. If you will just sit quietly in the back of the room and read these magazines, I won't bother you. And if anyone wants to learn anything about anything, then come up front and I'll teach you whatever you want to learn."

I waited for them to move to the back or front of the room. But they just sat there, silently, eighteen hulking guys in little tab-arm chairs, staring at me. "Just move your chairs," I said. "It's really okay. I won't give you a failing grade. You just need to sit quietly in the back so I can teach whoever wants to learn anything up here in the front." They still didn't move. They didn't speak. They didn't look at each other. I felt they were embarrassed to move while I was looking at them. So I said, "Okay, I'll turn around and then you can move to the back or the front."

I turned around and instantly, without their saying a word to each other, there was a loud noise as the chairs moved. Then silence. I thought, "Oh, no. They have all moved to the back. It's over for me."

I turned to them and saw they had all pushed their chairs up to my desk, as close and as jammed together as possible. We looked at each other, into each other's eyes. Time stopped. Something happened to us.

After wiping away my tears with my fingers, I asked them what they wanted to learn. They wanted to learn how to read and write. When we began our work, I found out they were almost illiterate. "How did you get to the ninth grade?" "They always just passed us on. They don't care about us."

Over the rest of the semester I read to them, had discussions with them, taught them some grammar and some writing. They worked hard, were angels, and learned. What had changed? What had happened? I had discovered that by not being the boss but, instead, by putting myself in the service of their desire to learn, our hearts and minds and spirits opened up and a community was born in which teaching and learning could occur.

I also discovered that some worked quickly and broadly and kept wanting more challenges, while others worked slowly and deeply and kept wanting more time for reflection. I felt that if they were separated into two classes, one in which some could speed along from challenge to challenge and one in which others could stop and reflect along the way, it would be easier for us. So, without discussing it with the students, I talked to the teacher who had the other "loser" class and asked her if one of us could have all the "slow" students and the other all the "fast" students the second semester. She agreed, if she could have the "fast" students. And so the students were divided.

Her slow students—actually her trouble-makers—came into our community like barbarians and my civilized students went into her class as into exile. After the semester started, Danny Severino, one of the fast students, came to me and asked, "Why did you give us away? Did we do something wrong?" I tried to reorganize the class, but the principal wouldn't let me rectify the situation. I mention Danny's name as a memorial; he soon dropped out of school and a few years later died of a drug overdose. Was it my fault? Even partly my fault? It is important for me to think so, because it keeps me aware of how sensitive and precious every student is.

I learned my second lesson at the school I went to as a literature and history teacher after my temporary job at the public school ended. It was a private school for rich, high-IQ high-school drop-outs. Their parents paid a lot of money to keep their children in this school of last resort. And the owners of the school made sure the children stayed there—by having classes no larger than ten students, by letting students walk out of any class any time they felt like it, and by paying the teachers by how many students were in each class each day.

Here I learned that when students have the freedom to accept or reject how their teacher is teaching, they aren't disruptive trouble-makers; instead, they simply get up and walk out. It was a chilling experience when students looked into my eyes as I was lecturing and I could see they were thinking, "This means nothing to me," after which, quietly and politely, they picked up their books and left the room. Through trial and error I eventually learned that when I told them what I really thought and felt, asked them what they thought and felt, told them when I wasn't sure, and invited them to help seek the truth, they stayed and talked and thought, worked hard, were angels, and learned.

In this school, for example, I learned, with and from the students, more about American history than I had ever learned from the textbooks I had studied unquestioningly in school. But the students refused to use those books: "One reason I dropped out of my old high school was because of these stupid books. They're so completely superficial." The students wanted to study "the real story." So we used primary sources and they struggled with them—and a community was born in which teaching and learning could happen.

Rich students, working-class students, white students, minority students—they were all the same; they all wanted to learn, but they all needed teachers who respected them.

The third lesson took several years and many experiences to learn. It started one day about twelve years ago when I was standing in front of my college developmental writing students, not understanding why these intelligent adults who desired to learn could not grasp the simplest grammar concepts. I had tried many different workbooks and methods, but nothing worked. I respected them and we had a community—but since learning wasn't happening, I had to conclude that teaching wasn't happening either. In light of our mutual frustration, I finally stopped the grammar lesson one day and said to them, "I know you are smart. I know you know how to learn because you know how to do a lot of things. How did you learn those things? How *do* you learn? Can you think of one thing you know how to do well and tell me how you learned it?" Yes, they could. "Okay, I said. "Write down how you learned to be good at that thing. Just say what you did from when you first started learning it to when you got to be good at it."

When they were finished writing, I asked them what they had done at the start of their learning, and I wrote everything they said on the board. They called out a number of different things, including "start basic" and "practice"; and then the flurry of responses died down. "And then?" A third flurry, including "more practice," "felt more comfortable and confident."

"Is that it or is there more?" A fourth flurry, including "keep it going," "knowing what the results will be," "creative." I asked whether they had anything else and there was a fifth flurry, including "becomes second nature," "improvement." When that flurry died down, I asked again, "Is this the end or is there more?" A sixth—and last—flurry, including "mastering it," "teaching it."

When I stepped back from the board to look at their six stages, my scalp prickled: These were similar to the six stages of learning that Piaget had discovered as the stages by which infants learn every concept and skill from birth to about eighteen months. "Can there be a natural, innate human learning process that starts at birth and continues through life?" I asked myself.

I began to ask students in all my courses, both the developmental and the college transfer courses, to write down how they had learned something outside of school that they are good at doing. They all reported similar stages in a similar sequence. Then I began to ask teachers at conferences— with the same results (by now I have asked more than 2,000 people—all with the same results). So I began trying to develop curriculum and instructional methods that would create, in the classroom with school subjects, this natural human learning process. At the heart of this natural learning process approach, as reported by over 2,000 learners, are such elements as doing authentic, meaningful work; making and learning from one's own mistakes; and being creative.

I began experimenting with these natural human learning process elements, trying to incorporate more and more of them into the curriculum: for example, having students do their own writing rather than using workbooks; giving them challenging writing tasks that invite creative and critical thinking; starting where they are and focusing on constructing a foundation upon which higher-level knowledge can then be constructed; knowing they need to practice, practice, practice; viewing mistakes as opportunities for learning; providing for the highest possible level of individual activity and small group inter-activity. My students began learning the grammar concepts; they began improving their writing; they became intellectually energized. For example, here are excerpts from a pre-test and a post-test written by a man in his 20's who had been brain-damaged during a childhood illness. The writing prompt was the same for both tests: "Write about one of your best classes." All errors have been retained.

> *Pre-test:* The best class I toke in high school was radio communication. it consisted of having good attendance and we had to take class notes but the teacher would only make us write notes that were on the board, we would watch movies every Friday. . . .

> *Post-test:* The best class that I had taken in high school was radio communication. The way I found out about the class was from the student's school Directory that was given to me by my counselor. I was reading the Directory in my counselor's office when my Dad and I were there. . . .

Here is another example, excerpts from pre- and post-tests written by a returning student in her 30's. The prompt for the pre-test was the same as I had used for the first student's class; the prompt for the post-test for this second student's class, however, was to respond to a moral dilemma concerning a student about to graduate from college, having to get ready for graduate school, and who, because of lack of time, had cheated on a writing assignment and was now facing expulsion. Again, all errors have been retained.

> *Pre-test:* I liked the class because I new most of the people in it. the Teacher was very good he made it interesting and fun. . . . The atmosphere was great it was fun and at times it was serious. . . . You got to act out important parts in history.

> *Post-test:* Mike should have started his paper a lot earlier because he knew he would have a lot of things to do to get ready for graduate school. The teacher should try to understand all the pressure Mike was going through, rather than expell him from school. I think they should give him another chance provided that he knows about the plagiarism rule. . . .

These illustrate the kind of progress developmental writers now make in one quarter in my classroom, the classroom of a teacher whose students have taught her how to teach. What have they taught me? That students have a powerful desire to learn; that students have an innate and natural learning process; and that when this is taken into account in curriculum and teaching methods, students become successful learners; that students must be respected; that the classroom can be a community. They taught me how to help them become empowered. And I thank them for these gifts.

My Most Fulfilling Experience as a Teacher

Leslye Friedberg, Community College of Philadelphia

Walking to class on a chilly day last February, I spotted Tamara coming toward me, peeking around the shoulder of another student. Through the crush of backpacks and winter coats, we locked hands. "Great to see you!" we blurted, laughing in unison. Urged on by the crowd and our destinations, our hands slipped apart. "Say hi for me if you see the others," I said, turning back, already missing her smile. I continued on, wishing as I had on other days that I were headed to our old classroom. They'd all be there, again—Tamara Ford, Ann Fusco, Hector Lopez, Trina Clark, David Wilson, Belinda Lloyd, Ann Scott, Ingrid Madrid, Maria Torres, Tammi Turner . . . names worth repeating . . . faces I don't forget. I think of them constantly. It's been that way since the day we met.

After eight years of teaching college—from the serene Ohio campus where I strolled flowered paths with Ursuline nuns, to the security-guarded buildings in downtown Philadelphia—I still can't shake my first-day dread. Even after meeting hundreds of students, I'm always nervous. Sure, there have been lots of wonderful ones: the small-town mayor with tattoos on her arms; the cop who wins *Star Trek* look-alike contests; the self-proclaimed hood who charmed me with Shakespeare and Blake. Others, however, haunt me: the anonymous scribbler whose cryptic notes accused me of Satanic affiliation; the woman who praised me and told me I reminded her of her daughter and then filed a grievance charging me with discrimination against older women.

As the hour draws near and I have to walk into a new classroom, I've often gotten myself into a state, imagining some calamity that could spoil the mood for the duration. Don't get me wrong. I'm optimistic, generally. But when you teach required courses, you quickly learn that one or two unhappy students can set the tone for the whole class. My expectations about classes are a lot like my expectations about my hair. Every morning I wake up hoping my hair will look like Isabella Rossellini's. It has, a few times. Most days it resembles Lyle Lovett's, and that's okay, really. But other days I awake to Medusa. There's no way to predict it. I make the best of it, but I can't forget my ideal. Classes are like this too. A disgruntled wrestler who thinks he should be in an honors class commandeers three seats in front and glares at me for the whole semester. A woman tangled in a Sports Walkman rushes in clutching a list of eleven days she can't be in class and asks, "Will this be a problem?" Two more lounge in the rear snickering behind their hands, snapping their gum. I tell myself they'll stop soon. They're having withdrawal from tanning booths and *All My Children.* I make it a point to say something *extra* pleasant as I call the roll. I notice on the class list that they're nursing majors. If I'm not nice to them, one day I'll be in a hospital bed and. . . . I stare at the class list until the print blurs.

Then, it starts. Out of the corner of my eye, I see one of me creep toward the blackboard, then relax in the corner with a cup of coffee. "What's wrong? You've done this before. You lived. Don't let things irritate you. Relax . . . ree-lax. I'll be back, but not while you're irritable like this." That half eventually edges back and we're integrated, but then I blow it again somehow. It's like Don Quixote and Sancho Panza. Together, they complement each other; apart, they languish. When my saner self departs, the unsteady me sees windmills in every student's eyes.

But this class was different. This class was an Isabella Rossellini hair day. Who knows what alchemy was in the air. Or why the campus copy service lost my syllabus that morning, forcing me to abandon my first-day rituals. Maybe after all, it *was* serendipitous that I got my course assignment only two days earlier, had never taught this particular remedial course, and had no idea what kind of students I would find. I had to improvise. I arrived early with my only prop, a favorite Langston Hughes poem, "Theme for English B." The real magic started when they walked into the room, exchanging smiles, timid, unsure of what would happen next. I knew the feeling.

"This class is for dummies, isn't it?" Ann Scott asked matter-of-factly. I'd heard different versions of this question, but her bluntness took me by surprise. I couldn't bear to hear myself mouthing the standard speech, calm and reasoned, explaining the importance of knowing the basics before trying harder classes and how everyone is better at some subjects than others. It rarely convinces anyone. They stared at me, waiting for my answer, expecting confirmation of what they already believed. I looked at them, at their fresh spiral notebooks and new backpacks, at the eagerness marred by uncertainty. Whoever made them feel like dummies, I thought to myself, churning, gave them a fear of beginning anything, made them envision failure instead of promise. I hated that.

"You know," I said, inspecting the printout, "my class list says this is English 089/097, Fundamentals of Reading and Writing. I don't see the word *dummy* on here anywhere." They glanced at each other. I bit the inside of my cheek to keep from smiling. I looked back at the list more intently, shaking my head. "Nope, not one mention of dummy." They saw my smile break. "So, how'd you like to read a poem?" I asked. By then, we were all smiling so hard that I swear it looked like the sun had come drifting over our windowless room.

We read Hughes's poem. They didn't complain about it being too old or that it doesn't rhyme. They liked what he said to them.

"This is *deep*," Trina began.

That made me smile.

"Why you laugh?" she asked me. "I mean it."

"It is," Belinda confirmed. "It's really *deep stuff*."

That became their highest compliment to a writer, when something really impressed them, moved them, made them see things in a new way. They didn't bestow this honor casually, and every time one of them said it, I felt happy.

Once we started talking about that poem and about ourselves, we never stopped. "As I learn from you/I guess you learn from me," Hughes, the young student, tells his college instructor. We agreed that was the best part.

In the next days, we discussed how this class could make a real difference. They knew, only too well, what was riding on it. They had to pass this course plus one more remedial course before they could take Freshman English. Most of them had never written paragraphs before, let alone an essay. But the biggest problem was their lack of self-confidence. Their honesty and willingness amazed me. When David bravely offered, "It's in my head but I can't get it on paper," he summed up what many of them were feeling. They said teachers never asked them to write how *they* felt about anything. I remember Tammi, nonplussed, thinking she hadn't heard an assignment correctly: "So you mean you want me to write down how *I* feel about this character?" I nodded. She shook her head, exasperated with me. "Well, is there a *right* answer?" This time, I shook my head. Even when they did well, they wouldn't believe it. "I passed this test? You're not kiddin'?" They rolled their eyes when I assured them they'd be writing paragraphs in no time. Their determination made me work harder than ever. Their honesty made me more honest.

Seeing each other for two hours on Mondays, Wednesdays, and Fridays, we quickly fell into our own comfortable style. Coke cans, pretzel bags, papers, and books cluttered the desks. The circle of chairs became a jumble of pairs and threesomes. Frequently, our discussions erupted into wild, unrelated asides: fashion updates, crime reports, lessons in childrearing. On more than one afternoon, I ran around the room gesturing the referee time-out signal, except I'd shout, "Tangent, tangent . . . you guys are off on another tangent!" The first time I did this, they became mute, stunned; after that, they simply put up with me as if I were the proverbial crazy aunt. My favorite days were Fridays. That's when Tamara's four-year-old nephew came with her. (Otherwise, she explained, she'd have to stay home to babysit.) I balked at this at first, insisting he would be a distraction. Actually, he was . . . we enjoyed watching him fall asleep on two chairs pushed together, his crayons and manila paper on the floor. When I closed the door of our room, I forgot the racket of 17th Street, forgot the departmental memos about managing classroom conflict and racial tensions. Not once was there a trace of animosity among us, never a disparaging remark. For those two hours, we had a world that not only worked; it thrived. When 3:20 came, I didn't want them to go.

One day I started class saying, "I was telling a friend of mine about you and. . . ."

Ann Fusco interrupted me: "You talk about *us* to people?"

"Yes, I answered, genuinely surprised. "I talk about you a lot. . . . This class is the highlight of my day!"

"You better get a life," Ann joked, dismissing me with a wave.

I wanted to hear what they thought about everything. While I watched a production of *The Colored Museum*, a play I knew they'd love, I dreamed them into the audience beside me, saw them nudging each other and laughing. When I went to the record store, I wondered what they'd pick. I wanted to sit in their kitchens with the aunts, mothers, and children they wrote about. Everywhere I went, I imagined them with me.

In reality, we did go to two college activities together. The first, a play about the trial of William Penn, I remember not so much because of its dramatic or historic value, but because it was the inspiration for the very first paragraphs my students wrote. Their landmark paragraphs reflected victories no less important than the one Penn enjoyed. Our second adventure took us to the campus career placement services office. I still can't believe I proposed this seemingly boring field trip. Even these students, so agreeable to everything, would think I was a nerd. But it seemed like an opportunity for them to be more involved in the college and to see that their goals really were attainable.

"Don't you think it'd be fun to visit the career placement office?" I queried, as if I were asking them to a party. "I just met the director and she invited us."

"Sure," they said. "What is it?"

As it turned out, nothing about our visit was boring. We played with new computer programs that select careers corresponding to your personality. We huddled around the colorful screens, eager to learn our destinies. In fact, the computer informed me that I might be better suited for a career as a surgeon. That made the trip intriguing for me, but when the week ended and my students produced their first essays—three whole paragraphs focused on a possible major and some careers that might follow—I gave up any notions of trading in my pencil for a scalpel.

Weeks into writing this essay, I was struggling, especially with the introduction, which I'd changed three times. I didn't think I'd be able to write it. One afternoon, wondering how I'd ever get it right, I heard a familiar voice sound my name. It was Maria, coming from her English class.

"I've been thinking about you," I said, relieved to see her. "I'm trying to write this essay about our class, and it's hard."

"Oh, I *know*," she commiserated, "it's not easy to write about things you're close to. I'm writing about my brothers."

"I can't get my introduction right," I sighed.

And then, in a voice of experience, Maria advised me, "So, do what you always told us," she said, seeing I'd forgotten the obvious. My eyes grew big. "If you can't do your introduction right away, don't get stuck there . . . work on another part. You'll figure it out later."

"Did I say that?" I grinned, embarrassed yet honored that a student remembered my words.

We started towards the parking garage, rejuvenated.

"Hey," she added, resting a hand on my shoulder, "you need any more help, call me."

We made progress. Fragments grew into sentences. Sentences combined into paragraphs. That's not to say it was always easy. We had our days. And, I admit, there were times when my body-split problem recurred. Like the day when I'd explained topic sentences five different ways and couldn't think of a sixth. I launched into one of the all-time trite lectures known to students throughout history: "You guys aren't working hard enough. Did you really do your homework? Because it explains what a topic sentence is." Suddenly, with gale-force velocity, half of me flew back against the blackboard, deserting the frustrated-teacher part of me. In my peripheral vision, I saw the other me, dazed and wobbly, stars circling her head. "Ohhhhh," she moaned, checking her head for blood, "WHY did you do that?"

Ingrid slowly raised her hand. "Are you mad at us, Leslye?"

"No," I said, averting my eyes, like a misbehaved puppy. "Sorry, I. . . ."

"The reason you use a topic sentence. . . ." Hector intervened in his deep, serious tone, explaining it better than I ever did.

Slowly my other half edged back toward me, wary. "Don't do that again, okay?"

All in all, I was pretty well-behaved. By the end of the semester, my kinetic malady was under control, not entirely gone, but treatable. It's what they gave me that helped most. Because they were themselves, they let me be myself. No, they *invited* me to be myself, whatever that was on any day—

impatient, excited, silly, or serious. What a thrill to walk into a classroom with people who like being there and who want you there. They were looking for more than a teacher; they wanted a person. And so they got the best and the most I'd given to any class, more than I suspected I had. They weren't looking for A's, or easy answers, or a return on their cash investment. They wanted a reason to go on, to know they could. Frankly, that's exactly what I'd been needing too. A good reason to think I could go on teaching. I found it, and in the most unexpected place.

When my students' final essays were evaluated by two other faculty members, all of them passed. I tore out of the building waving their blue books like a flag, dodging cars and students, and into the student center to our planned celebration spot. Of course, they barely believed me when I screamed, "You passed! You did it!" They thumbed through their blue books looking for verification. Even then, they were a little hesitant to accept the good news. But after we broke open the boxed cupcakes and tacos, and were reminiscing about those days before they'd written a paragraph, they were proud about how far they'd come. They knew they'd made it. There we were for one last afternoon together, everything right, exactly like the day we met, only better.

These days, whenever I feel that first-day dread, I just think of those students. Then, I walk into any classroom knowing I can do it. I keep myself together. And if there's a moment when I don't, I'll know I'll get over it. I remember everything they gave me. The really deep stuff.

How I Learned to Teach While Learning to Learn on the Rollerblade Trail

Stephanie Packer, Miami-Dade Community College

Like most of my colleagues, I have taken various methods and educational philosophy courses. In spite of my expectations, they weren't fatal; I actually learned useful things. But, more because of my limitations than the material's, the things I learned remained utilitarian, functional, external to the way I really looked at the world. They were techniques that let me glide more smoothly through the day and made the going-home time come sooner. Eventually I accumulated quite a repertoire of these tricks to keep students happy and filling out those positive evaluation forms, all without my having to work harder. Frankly, that was key, the not-working-harder part.

It's not that I hated my job. On the contrary, I found the life quite pleasant, especially with the addition of the latest crisply packaged new methods gizmos which I would eagerly unpack after each workshop or conference. I liked my job, but I suspected it was unnecessary, particularly in non-developmental classes. After all, like most people who grew up to be college professors, academic learning came naturally to me. In the right-brained pursuits, I never really felt having a teacher was essential, and in the left-brained pursuits, I was content to remain a respectful stranger.

So, by whatever perverse calculus undergirds things worldly, I specialized in that for which I felt no need of a teacher and eventually became that unneeded teacher myself. All the while I guiltily guarded the fiction of my necessity. In effect, my construction of the situation meant that I was wedded to a meaningless role. Isn't hubris always punished? The gods had the last laugh on me when, well over the age of forty, I was seized by the mad desire to take up rollerblading.

From the first day I became a learner in an area I was none too confident in, my perspective changed. I grew up a bookworm, not a jock, but for months, years actually, I had dreamed of skating like the wind. There was something in the motion that I wanted, not mere exercise, but little vacations from being earthbound. I soon discovered a new admiration and respect for our underprepared students who struggle to overcome the limitations of their prior experience because they want more from themselves and their lives.

Finally, fueled by my husband Arthur's endless store of encouragement, I nerved myself to buy some skates and protective gear. At last came the first day of school and my maiden voyage . . . or not. Skating like the wind, was it? What had I been thinking? I stayed frozen on the coconut mat outside the front porch, skates pristine and likely to remain so as I crouched in the hilariously misnamed "ready" stance. Arthur stood by as spotter. And stood. Potential spotter is perhaps a more apt description here. I looked in his eyes with a heartfelt glance that said, "The skates are going straight back to the store." I was very close to quitting before I ever got started, but if I didn't find a way to enter this new dimension, the dream was over, and my life would be poorer. As a teacher, I had never been much of a first-day pep talker, but since that experience, I devote much of the first few meetings of developmental courses to motivational and confidence-building activities. Otherwise, students, like me, may quit before ever getting started.

Eventually Arthur, a natural teacher, did coax me up and down the front walk, a grand total of perhaps forty feet, all the while praising me extravagantly. The second lesson was more of the same, just getting minimally comfortable with the new stance and world of uncertainty. Could I have overcome my fear and started gaining basic skills without his help and encouragement? Absolutely not. Hmmmm. Perhaps my life as a teacher was not the pleasant but useless role I imagined. At the end of the first two lessons, I realized that certain conditions important to acquiring new skills applied to the cognitive as well as to the physical domain. The list includes the following:

Commitment. I had a lot invested in the dream, both in dollars and in fantasy. It would have been worse to renounce the dream than to risk getting off the coconut mat. It would have cost me too much to fail. Similarly, students, especially developmental students, need to commit to their dreams and goals in a deeper way than simply enrolling in school necessarily implies. They also need to value learning and have too much invested in their project to consider quitting when the magnitude of what they have asked of themselves becomes apparent. Enrolling in school is just buying the skates, and the skates, those first few days, can always be sent back to the store.

Praise. All the methods courses had taught me the importance of praise, but beyond a point, I found it patronizing. Now that I had become a developmental roller skater, I soaked up every bit of this encouragement as a necessity. So do my students need praise, and not only for "big" things. That first step off the mat takes courage.

Trust. I had to trust my spotter when he said it would be OK if I got off the mat, that he would support me down the walk. How confident students feel with our direction and intentions really matters. Assuming competence, our true attitude to students may be more important than which program we sign on to.

Small achievable steps. Gliding like the wind was such a far distance from where I started that I had to break down the project into smaller units, little victories. The day I got out of the front yard on my own power represented tremendous progress, though that would have been obvious to no one but Arthur and me. It wasn't necessary to do a whole lot more that day. Although the educational theory classes espouse the notion of a limited number of new skills at one time, I tended not to have much patience with an exquisitely slow pace, or what I privately thought of as "spoon-feeding" students. Now I know what it feels like to be attempting an endeavor for which little in one's previous experience has prepared one. It's all too apparently "logical" to give up.

In developmental writing classes, my area, this translates into having students write paragraphs concentrating on one skill at a time, gradually building up the full range; for example, first subject-verb agreement, then subject-verb agreement and avoiding fragments, then those two skills plus possessives, and so forth. If I had expected all or nothing as a skater those first few lessons, I would have ended up with nothing.

Then came the next phase of my developmental learning, when the "easy" preliminaries were over and it was time for serious business. Lessons three through seven were the heart of my learning, similar to weeks three through twelve of a fourteen-week semester, where the hard, grubby work of mastering basic skills gets done. This intermediate stage yielded up its own insights that made me see classroom learning from a different perspective— the learner's.

Magic formula. By lesson three, my innocence had worn off and I had some sense of what I was in for, but no sense of what I could do to bridge the frightening gulf of my skating illiteracy. I see that same consciousness of impending doom in my students' eyes when the work of college starts to overwhelm them. I still was terrified to leave the coconut mat and start rolling, so Arthur told me to birdwalk off the mat, feet at right angles in a V.

This saved the life of my project. "Bird-bird, bird-bird, bird-bird" became my comic but enabling mantra. Uttering its reassuring familiarity, I was finally able to birdwalk, then slowly roll down the front sidewalk. In fact, I used the bird-mantra to nerve myself to begin each of the next five lessons. Dumb, but effective.

A small enabling formula can do wonders for learners as they make that first—and second and third—scary plunge. Whether it's a generic opening for the essay, a brainstorming formula, the FANBOYS mnemonic device for coordinating conjunctions, or the bird-mantra, I began to experience the importance to the underprepared and insecure learner of something which seemed to cut the odds, something certain and ritualistic to hold on to in a realm in which one knows oneself to be a stranger.

Gradually diminishing effort. The earlier lessons were more physically demanding than the later ones. At first, anxious about falling, I leaned forward in full-power position at all times, causing quite the inflamed lumbar region. How was I going to be able to sustain this for the thirty- or sixty-minute skates I envisioned? But as I gained experience and some confidence in this new dimension, I was able to relax more, and I found I didn't have to make such an all-out effort all the time.

I began to counsel struggling students that it's not always this hard, that we go through learning nodes when the stress of trial and error, engraving new neural pathways, just the grubby work of skills acquisition, is more of a strain than the future use thereof will be. Of course, we have to keep using the new skills, but it's easier to maintain and gradually build than to start.

Frequency of lessons. After a Saturday lesson, my skating receptors had been saturated, and I wasn't really ready to absorb more on Sunday. When I could manage a Monday or Tuesday session, though, rather than waiting a whole week, my progress was more rapid.

The physical domain is not identical to the cognitive one, and it's dangerous to draw simplistic one-to-one parallels in all cases. However, other experiences in the classroom also cause me to question the efficacy of weekly, or daily, compressed-term classes for developmental skills subjects.

The Gulf War principle. Don't declare victory too soon. By the end of my seventh lesson, I had "learned," or so I thought, until I missed a few weeks, then went out to skate and felt I had to learn everything from scratch. Actually, it was more a "re-booting" process, but it made me appreciate the volatility of recently acquired skills. The teaching implications point to the need for continued, after-the-course practice.

The eighth and ninth lessons were a time for consolidation and reinforcement, and perhaps a bit of experimentation. At this point, I could enjoy contemplating my expanded universe of possibilities.

The conclusions I came to were not particularly startling. In fact, they surprised me mainly by echoing some of the hoary tenets of educational philosophy I had dismissed as too transparently manipulative, cheerleaderish, patronizing, or bloodcurdling. What changed for me was the different way I understood those tenets now, having experienced the perspective of a developmental learner. Reconstituting one's world, or learning, is a precious and fragile aspiration that can be scared off by the sudden wrong move. I began to wonder whether I had also underestimated the contribution all my former teachers had made to my cognitive independence.

Other things have changed for me too. While previously the emphasis was on how soon I could go home, now I wonder how early I can get to work. I no longer schedule personal appointments for directly after work, because I know I'll never leave in time. And even once I do get home, there's a whole new on-line universe of resources and colleagues with whom to share them. I guess I just have a lot more respect for what my colleagues and I do now.

Having "learned" how to skate, I have by no means become a master. Rather, like my successful developmental students, I am just at the threshold, having mastered the basic skills necessary to become an independent learner. I'm under my own steam. Arthur is my companion and the trail is my teacher, and each session yields new lessons. I own my learning and it's limited only by energy and desire. Isn't this exactly what we want for our students?

The world I have is changed. It is a text I can re-read for missed nuances. Where before I saw merely roads or pathways, now I scan surfaces seeking the choice black silk of young asphalt, radar out for sudden potholes, loose macadam. The world as I knew it has yielded up hidden and uncontemplated dimensions. So our students, when they leave us, can see previously unsuspected richness and possibility in their worlds.

The world I can have is also changed. Now I can experience diverse moments not just as my old self, with the same tired pool of skills, but as a skater, with expanded competencies and possibilities I had thought of as belonging only to other people. Now I can be a skater who might take up skiing, or ice skating, or even scuba diving. These things, once unimaginable, are newly within my power. So is the world of dreaming and achieving for many of our students. Perhaps being a teacher is not just a middle-class scam after all.

Funny, I thought I was only learning how to rollerblade that day six months ago when I stood at the brink of the known world. In reality, I was learning how to learn, to marvel, and, I hope, to teach.

Kim Ordinary

Tom Riordan, John Jay College

She spoke loudly and often, always chewing gum, and she laughed and played around a lot. She dyed her hair a shade of gold just slightly lighter than her butterscotch skin. Her writing was unremarkable—brash, spirited, grammatically unorthodox. She was a lovely young woman, but that did not make her stand out. There are many lovely young students here. They are among New York City's brightest and hardest-working. Many come from housing projects where kids grow up both fighting or dreaming, and John Jay's students would never have made it to college at all if they did not do both well.

Somewhere inside each of these grown-up children are little, hidden cupboards crammed with old Spam cans and Miracle Whip jars filled with adamant gems and angelic liqueurs. Sometimes, I earn the privilege of being shown one of these cupboards. More rarely, one of their doors is opened for me and a jar or can is pointed out and its history told to me. More rarely still, I can pick one of the gems out and hold it up to the light, or carefully lift one of the liqueurs to my nose. These are the exquisite moments of being a teacher, and the most dangerous. I must not covet the gem; I must not put the liqueur to my lips.

After the first day of class, I could not have guessed that Kim was the student who would be unforgettable. This is not left up to me. The times I do say, "There's a young man whom I really want to know," often he turns out to be the one student that I don't ever connect with. He senses my desire. Like all students—like all children, grown or otherwise—he can sense when a teacher wants something *from* him, and he withdraws. But Kim simply struck me as an ordinary student. There was nothing that I wanted, beyond teaching her.

I would be too ashamed to write about it if I fell in love with Kim. This is not a story of crossing *that* line. Even admitting a fantasy of romance with a student would be too embarrassing. But if you sense a whiff of carnal romance somewhere in the air, your nose is not mistaken. Kim and another man were lovers, had been serious lovers for a long time, and had even tried to have a baby. Kim had gone to see a doctor, questioning her fertility. Then they changed their minds when she began college.

Unfortunately, what happened next is what often happens when a child of the ghetto goes to college. She changed subtly, or those back home imagined that she did. Since they loved her, they tried to pull her back to them. And so, one night, her lover left his condom off again, with the vague idea in the back of his head that if she did get pregnant, she would then leave college and return to being the doting high-school girl she used to be. On that night, Kim got pregnant. Ten weeks later, looking every bit as ordinary as she first had in January, she was standing in my office, her eyes wet. She sat down, burst into tears, and blurted out, "I'm pregnant and you have to tell me what to do!"

I did not want wet eyes in my office. I already had wet eyes inside my own head and inside my wife's head back at home. She and I too had been trying to have a baby, and had been to see a dozen doctors. Four years later, now well over 40 and still childless, we were dreaming about adoption, but running into different kinds of roadblocks there, too.

Now, suddenly, I saw Kim differently. I focused in on her in a way I hadn't before. In the same moment, of course, I lost all focus—lost all sight of her. Kim Ordinary girl was suddenly Kim Magical, Kim Risky, Kim Promising, Kim Victimized. It was not the boyfriend who victimized her, although he had walked out— "went on vacation from me," she said. He had not told her what to do or what he wanted her to do. He didn't know, I guess. He had wished her to be pregnant just to bring her down a notch off her high college horse. He was as terrified as she was of a baby. No, I was the victimizer. I wanted her baby. I could feel it in my throat, as big as a chair. I eyed her appraisingly: Kim Young, Kim Healthy, Kim Intelligent, Kim Pretty.

Could I do it? Was it a violation of the teacher-student bond if I told her, "It would be a dream come true for my wife and me if you let us adopt your baby." How *big* a violation?

I don't even think that I heard most of what she said. No, I must have heard, but not remembered. I was so humming with so many schemes, moral gyrations and rationalizations that my long-term memory sealed itself off, out of demure consideration for the future. The only other thing that I remember, really, was something she said about her tummy, a bikini, and a Spring Break trip to Cancun with her friends. I remember thinking, "How in God's name does she get the money for a Spring Break fling in Mexico?" I thought, "If this is her big worry, then I am justified in counseling her to give the baby up. She isn't ready."

All the while, she sat there, really broken-hearted—and I barely saw it. The tears rolled down her smooth, gold cheeks and fell onto her stylish black knit blouse. Her hair was cinched back and then spread loose again by one of those crinkly, lacy, multi-colored hair loops that they sell along the sidewalk so cheaply that I almost bought one for my wife, even though it was unlikely she would wear it. Kim chewed her gum more slowly now. Her eyes were ice blue. "Tom, what should I *do*?" she pleaded, sitting forward, pressing her clenched-together hands into the space between the knees of her expensive bleach-streaked jeans. What she wanted and expected as advice from me was one five-letter word, "Abort," but that word too was sealed off—trapped in the tar-pits of my mind.

I *could* do it. I saw that. If I broke some spun-glass cordon of good ethics, I would gladly put my hand out afterward to be slapped—but a father. This was something God had dropped in all our laps. Why mislabel serendipity as breach of confidence? Did Moses's mother say, "I can't," when Pharaoh's daughter hired her to wet-nurse the infant boy she had found in the bulrushes? Did she say, "There's a conflict of interest"?

So I nodded and told Kim how badly I felt for her. I said that I knew that she would make the best decision even though it might mean pain or sacrifice. I volunteered to walk her upstairs to a counselor I knew. "Whatever you do, I'll support you," I said. On the way upstairs, a dozen plans flew through my mind—a dozen ways to manipulate the situation and incline it toward adoption. At least, I would say that my wife and I were in the wings *in the eventuality* that Kim decided on adoption. I must not *deprive* her of an option by my silence. It might be the perfect choice for *her. That* would not be unethical at all.

Two years later, I still am running all those schemes through my mind because I never said a word about my wife and me. As we climbed the stairs, Kim turned her damp face to me, smiled weakly, put a finger to her chest and said, "Something in here told me I could trust you."

Why? I wanted to scold her.

"You seem like you would be somebody's father," she said.

By the time we reached the fifth floor, I had pushed that big chair back down my throat and made it return to the depressing waiting room with all of my and Joanna's other fruitless possibilities for parenthood, and sit still in it again. I felt, and I still feel, a light weight of satisfaction and a heavy weight of dull pain. I am not proud of it. A person is not proud of letting one dear thing drop so that he can hold tighter to a second dear thing. At first I thought that I had dropped the father to hold onto the teacher, but on second thought, I saw that Kim was right and that what I was doing was becoming the father, and dropping something else.

The next time I saw her, it was a year later, in the hallway. She had never returned to my class. Maybe she had sensed my desire to take something from her. Even though I had suppressed it, with her help, and done what I was supposed to do, maybe I had violated her anyway. Still, she was very happy to run into me. The crinkly hair loop was gone. She wore an ordinary, plain black band now, very much like what my wife Joanna wears.

She pulled my wrist. "How are the little ones?" she asked insistently, her blue eyes sparkling. "Oh, I *heard!*"

Joanna and I had two little babies at home. Our oldest, Grace, we had adopted in Poughkeepsie three days before Christmas. Seven weeks later, Joanna had given birth to Gabriel here in New York. Now, taped to my office door was a picture of the two infants sitting together, smiling and naked, in a large baby rocker.

"They're fine," I said.

"You should of *told* me!" Kim said. "I didn't *know!*"

"Know what?" I said.

"That you and your wife was—you know—looking for a *baby.* Anyway, I'm very glad to hear that you and her are finally *parents* now!"

"And how are you?"

"I dropped out."

"I noticed."

"I know I should of called you. That was very rude to not call back. But you know. It was very hard, what I had to do."

"Did you have an abortion?"

"Yes. You could guess that, right? Yeah, it was very painful to me to do that to a innocent baby, but I did it anyway. You know?"

"All the choices that you had were painful."

"I would never do that again, no matter what. Oh, Tom, you should of seen me! I *cried!*"

"I can imagine."

"No you can't! You can never imagine that thing."

"You're right."

"So, tell me, how are the babies? What are their *names?*"

"Grace is the girl and Gabriel is the boy."

"Oh, I want to see them! You and your wife got to invite me to come over sometime, okay?"

"That would be great."

"It's a deal then, right?" She smiled.

It was a good deal. She never came to visit, but there was really no need. She had survived and blessed us. The counselor upstairs had done her job, and Kim was back in college, slightly more grown up and less carefree but still enthusiastic about life. And I had survived and I bless her. In a time of drought, she had opened up her cupboard and taken down a little jar of bitter but sustaining liqueur for me. When I was so thirsty for fatherhood, she gave me an illicit taste of it that I will always remember. No, it isn't memory at all. I still can taste it.

We meet in the hallways now and then and shyly say hello. We remember all that happened and how intimate it was. We both did something wrong. In her youth, she let her own fears and desires eclipse some of her fetus's humanity, and in my age, I let my hopes eclipse her. We both crossed lines we shouldn't have; we both are maculate; but we are both to be forgiven, and we know it. The extraordinary thing—the brief visit by an angel—is over. The ordinary has returned and we both welcome it. Kim now has other people in her life to open cupboards for, and with my own two little cherubim at home now, so do I.

Most Influential Teacher: Mister B.

Marion B. Schafer,
New Hampshire Community/Technical College

Thirty years ago my classmates and I just had to smile when our eighth-grade English teacher stood on his desk to read aloud our writings, giving them no less authority than he gave the sentences of Scott, Dickens, and Twain. Fearlessly we wrote for the audience, for we knew Mister B. would be soliloquizing our pages like Richard Burton. He aimed to foster our confidence and our enjoyment of language, and, while he encouraged smiling, he shot anyone who ridiculed anyone else—he kept a banana in his desk drawer for that purpose.

"Bang!" he would say, pointing it at the offender.

Grammar, however, was tedious work: Mister B. taught us the parts of speech, and we diagrammed the structures of sentences.

We drew horizontal foundations for subjects and verbs. We partitioned off direct objects and other complements. We embellished our diagrams with hanging baskets: adjectives and adverbs, prepositional phrases and participles. We built towers to hold infinitives, and we constructed double- and triple-decked parking garages for parallel clauses, phrases, and modifiers. We annexed our main clauses with subordinate ones as we covered blackboard after blackboard with the soft, yellow-chalk designs of ideas.

We learned especially not to dangle modifiers—lying little words and phrases stuck onto the wrong things in a sentence: *Wanted: a piano by an old lady with carved legs.* Even though images of our fourth-grade music teacher played in our heads, we suspected that *with carved legs* probably misrepresented the truth. "Dang. mod.!" Mister B. cursed, beating the phrase from the board in clouds of yellow dust and relocating it near the piano. Sometimes he squeaked the chalk on purpose.

I loved Writing and Literature, but I thought Grammar was too structured, so when it was time to sign up for a high-school curriculum—either College Preparatory Scientific, which emphasized laboratories, or College Preparatory Classical, which emphasized languages—I chose Scientific.

When Mister B. asked why, I answered that I found grammar quite boring, thank you, and I had had enough. I thought science would be much more interesting. He accepted my reasoning without comment, even though he must have known that the choice would affect only my first year of high school. A new high school with a new curriculum was being built, and in our second year we would move into it, where he would be moving as well.

Four years later as a senior at that school, I found myself in Mister B.'s Writing class again, where I learned to write again. He didn't shoot the class with bananas, and he didn't make us diagram sentences. Instead, he made us purchase, read, and write in Strunk and White's *Elements of Style*, a book that does what it tells its readers to do, and does it cheerfully: "Every writer, by the way he uses the language, reveals something of his spirit, his habits, his capacities, his bias. This is inevitable, as well as enjoyable."

Enjoyable or not, we wrote a paper a day. For Mister B. that meant fifteen papers to read and comment on every night, and he did it faithfully. Sometimes the papers were terrible, but we cranked them out anyway. The important thing was, he kept us writing, kept us messing with words and sentences, kept us fearless and smiling. If I hadn't taken Writing, I would have taken physics, which met in the science lab during the same period. But I was moving too fast for calculations and lab reports. I enjoyed writing my own truths and telling them in other people's heads. I enjoyed having the last word. Writing was power I found nowhere else—and freedom.

It was freedom especially from the grades that governed my life in other classes. Mister B. did not grade our daily papers, so we were forced to pay attention to his comments, which were often humorous and less concerned with right and wrong than with making choices. He corrected language that needed it, but only selectively, and only to make points that might prove useful elsewhere. Had I noticed, for example, that although this was a sentence fragment, it probably worked better here than a complete sentence could have? Well, no. But I did the next time and every time after that.

What I did not understand until much later was that many of the others in my class were there not because they loved to write but because they hated to. This was one last chance for them to learn, far away from the required English courses they had to pass to graduate. Here they were safe: as long as they kept writing, they could do no wrong.

I also did not understand that besides teaching writing—or allowing me to learn for myself—Mister B. was also teaching how to teach writing, even to those who hate it.

Now I understand—that we write best about what we know and care about, that correction is useless without motivation, and that confidence in oneself, one's mind, and the power of one's words is what separates the writers from the typists. I understand also that most people have to enjoy writing or they'll talk on the phone instead. And I know all kinds of popular methods-phrases Mister B., now retired, probably never bothers with when he talks about old times: "writing process," "developmental writing," "conferencing," "portfolio evaluation," "multiple-drafting," "whole language," "writing workshops," "peer editing." Still he used those methods, every single one. According to most of my colleagues, thirty years ago was a dark age in the teaching of writing. Could have fooled me. That's when the light bulb came on in my little closet, and Mister B. was pulling the chain.

Still, I was haunted by sentence diagrams. Every time a new acquaintance discovered that I taught English, I was asked, "Do you make *your* students diagram sentences?" I always answered, "Nah, we don't do that any more. It's useless. In fact, we don't even teach grammar any more. We teach The Writing Process." My new ally would then rest assured that students these days have been spared.

Even though it was true that now and then I had drawn pictures to show students how basic structures convey meanings, I never drew the diagrams of eighth grade. They were too tedious, too complicated, and my experience proved it.

Until last fall, when after more than twenty years of teaching, I took a graduate course in language science at Harvard, where I was hoping to learn more about teaching writing. At the start of a lecture on syntax, my professor talked about Noam Chomsky's book *Syntactic Structures*, which I had read twice the week before. A book of arrows and parentheses, capitalized algebraic variables and Greek symbols, it is supposed to make sense of grammar and sentence structure. After two unsuccessful readings, I was confused, and I hated it. I sat in my chair, hanging my head.

"How many of you remember how to diagram sentences?" asked my professor.

Perking up, I raised my hand. A lot of other people raised theirs, too.

"Good," she said. "That's where we begin. . . ."

Starting with horizontal lines, she drew deep and surface sentence structures, turning them into upside-down, flowering sentence-trees on blackboard after blackboard, leading us among the branches of the structures we understood and into the concepts that had evaded us. I cringed. In quite the same way and for quite the same reason, though with much less sophistication, I had been diagramming sentences for my own students all along, but I had been misrepresenting the truth, lying to myself and to others. Here I was—an old lady with carved legs, dangling my modifiers, looking for a piano.

I have since mended my ways. I now understand that somehow or other The Writing Process must include learning to manipulate language structures, for on those structures ride our very ideas. The more structures we know how to use, the more choices we have, and the more we can say. Students in developmental writing classes have often missed or avoided experiences (some, tedious ones) that could have given them more structures to choose from, so they have no confidence about building bridges from their thoughts to the thoughts of others.

They hate to write.

When they are finally ready to learn that writing is less about right and wrong than it is about making choices, I say, "Each sentence makes a picture in your reader's head. The picture has a structure, and you can change the picture by adjusting the structure of your sentence. Watch this. . . ," and I sidle over to the blackboard to prove it. I diagram my students' sentences, dangling elaborate curlicues from base lines. Sometimes I write the sentences, diagram them, then illustrate them with stick-figures: Noam biting, a dog biting, Noam being bitten by a dog, a dog being bitten by Noam. I am not a very good artist, and my students have never heard of anyone named Noam, so they smile at the antics.

My students have never heard of Mister B., either. I don't carry a banana, and I don't have a desk big enough to stand on, but I do my best under the circumstances.

"Bang!" I say, pointing one finger at them and drawing more curlicues with the chalk. They just keep smiling.

The One-Room Schoolhouse at the Edge of My Mind

Ronald D. Block, Milwaukee Area Technical College

When I first started school, it was because my mother could not always find a baby-sitter. I was four years old, and she taught in the very image of a one-room country school, with a hand-bell on her desk and coat-hooks on the walls and a coal-burning stove in the back of the room. Now that I am thirty-eight, I find that I have never really left that school, although I now make my own office, often, out of a trunk of a car, teaching five classes at two colleges. I often think back on my mother's one-room school with the false nostalgia one has for another person's life. Of course, she often worked for, literally, dollars a month; and she kept the first year of her marriage to my father a secret, fearing she might lose her job. But she could also teach eight grades of students without moving far from her desk, and she could teach the same students as they graduated year to year, while I am among the ranks of the so-called scholar-gypsies: an adjunct professor, a part-time instructor, a teacher with a back-pack.

On some days, I teach—this year at least—at an expensive private school that fancies itself, if not the Harvard, at least the Notre Dame of the Midwest; but at other times of the day, I teach at a city college with "Tech" as a middle name that pays by the hour. At the private school, one of my ex-students is suing the university for three-quarters of a million dollars, an eventuality that began with my correcting how he spelled the name of a novel's central character. I suggested that such an error was a little "suspicious" and gave him a B, and he replied with a letter threatening that I might lose my job and find myself in legal deep water for my rash and "unprofessional" corrections. He also made a vague allusion to Humpty-Dumpty, which I took to be somewhat frightening, and so before the sleeping giant of the university woke up enough to remove him from my class, I taught for two weeks with a uniformed officer sitting outside my door.

About the same time, at "Tech," after meeting a class for the first time, I overheard a student complaining that her English teacher was making the class read stories about sex with animals. I listened to her some more, and I realized that she was talking about me. As she walked by, I got her attention—a little intimidated by the size of the cross around her neck—and I tried to explain the Frog-Prince Story wasn't really about sex with animals, not at least the way I was teaching it. Then she started to complain about the Ray Carver story I had them read, how it had the F-word in there someplace. She said she had complained about this to the Dean, saying, "What if my son would open that book?!" And the Dean had said, "Well, that's real life, that's how people talk," to which she said, "Don't tell me about real life! I was a coke addict for ten years!"

Now, after hearing those two stories, you might be wondering something like this: Aside from them happening to the same vagabond teacher, what is the connection between these two disconnected tales? And I might be forced to answer: Very little. Perhaps no real connection at all. In fact, as a basic writing teacher I might scribble in the margins, "Work on transition"; and I might then contemplate briefly the fact that we ask our students to maintain the classical unities of form when even our own lives do not preserve them.

In the case of both of these students, I never heard the end of the story. The ex-addict vanished, never to be seen again, and the complaints of my litigious student still languish in a legal limbo of his own making. As for me, I still dream of the one-room school. While my mother not only attended the weddings of her students and sometimes their funerals, I teach students to write conclusions when my experiences with these students almost never have them. Television is often blamed for not only the fragmentary nature of our students' attention spans but also for the discontinuous nature of our postmodern lives; but I would have to admit that a typical TV sitcom preserves the classical unities of time and space more than my teaching career has. At the private university mentioned above (henceforth to be called "Market University"), my students sometimes blur together, because they are amazingly homogeneous in terms of class, race, and religion. I see them for a semester and they vanish, and I sometimes fear that I will remember only the ones who step up to me and say, "You give me a C? My daddy's going to have you fired!" At Tech, I teach students who also come and go like phantoms, and they never mutter, "This visitation is but to whet thy almost blunted purpose."

Adding to the discontinuity is how different these two groups of college students are. My students at Market U. find it easy to praise the ideals of racial harmony from their same-alike island community. In general, they are pre-selected for their abilities to please teachers, although sometimes they turn angry if not downright rabid. At Tech, my students sometimes shock me with how blunt they are about the racial tensions in this city, and their suspicions about teachers are often kept well-intact from high school. While my students at Market are sometimes rebelling against the expectations of their professional class, my students at Tech have a day job, and they are quite often on the rebound from drug abuse and abusive marriages. While my Market students have "travelled abroad" although they are all quite young, my Tech students are often migrants without a green card or middle-aged with a pink slip.

I cannot say that I straddle these two worlds, just that I am divided between them. As I shuttle between campuses with my back-pack, fat with a diverse array of textbooks, I continue to think of how my mother once sat at a desk in that little schoolhouse, watching the next generation of her students grow up. She had her problems, but they were the problems of using the same textbooks year upon year until they fell apart, the problems of keeping the students from carving their initials beside the initials of their uncles and aunts. I tend to mythologize her experiences even though that school has long ago disappeared; but now that I think of it, that school was rendered obsolete because of the policy known as "consolidation." It's almost as though its own unities had finally swallowed it whole.

And this all brings me to my main point, which is that for many teachers like me the problem is not—in the current and somewhat arrogant phrase—to "create diversity in the classroom"; the problem is to adapt to it, to reeducate yourself constantly to it, to learn how to breathe diversity and sometimes adversity as a fish breathes water. This is perhaps especially true for migrant teachers. I now live in what has been called the most economically segregated city in the country, but previous to this, I taught in North Dakota, where many of my students came from dying little towns with populations hardly holding on to a couple hundred souls. Because North Dakota is a remarkably homogeneous place, I armed myself in my writing classes with rural metaphors and examples to explain to them, say, the difference between abstract and concrete language (or "bovine" and "black angus") or how to shape an introduction. ("Think of calling the cows home and herding them together when introducing your essay.")

But after taking a job at Market University, and then discovering my adjunct wages were not going to be able to cover the expense of a modest apartment in a lousy neighborhood, I took on a last-minute intermediate writing class at Tech's downtown campus. With hardly enough time to crank out a syllabus, there I stood the first night, not only the only person with a rural background, but also the only white male. And after collecting that first night's writing, I saw again that often repeated lesson of how language marks nothing if not all our differences: our cultural and racial differences, our class and gender differences.

It strikes me as more than merely ironic that the linking verb "to be" would be an emblem of many of our cultural divisions, and I would not be honest if I did not say that, right off, I could not help but feel that a black teacher could address this issue better than I. Was I to be the cultural relativist, i.e. a white man explaining the grammar and history of black English to a class of mostly African-Americans? Some voice in my head told me that the best course to take would be to acknowledge the wonderful diversity of American English, to acknowledge that standard English preserves ideology, but then to proceed to teach the language of the marketplace, the mother tongue of Market U. That, of course, would be the language expected if not required outright in cover letters, office memos, and other forms of practical writing. But, realistically, how was I even to teach my students this language when my own skills with language had hardly allowed me to move freely in the marketplace? The only way I could teach the fabled lingua franca would be to make sure none of my students would ever see me in my office, a 1974 Chevy with a hub-cap missing.

And here is another problem I thought about that first night: as a writing teacher, I often draw upon my experiences—no surprise there—to illustrate sample topic sentences, thesis statements, kinds of paragraphs and sentences. Out of what experience was I to draw my examples? Did I really have experiences that connect with the experiences of my new students? For teachers with tenure, these problems might be solved by building a gothic cathedral of a course year by year, or by attending another conference and carrying the gospel back; but for the teacher with a back-pack, rapid adjustments are necessary. Maybe I shouldn't even be in the classroom; maybe only those teachers whose departments pay for a trip to the Many C's Convention should be allowed to teach. But do not kid yourself: there are thousands of teachers like me, teachers who have more wit than theory. And I should add that I do about as well in the role of "teacher as *picaro*" as could be expected, even winning one teaching award that was usually reserved for the teachers who actually have their own offices. For those teachers like me, who have only the ruins of some increasingly figurative country schoolhouse at the edge of their mind, wit will have to do.

So I applied my wit to the problems I faced as I prepared to teach this new class, and the only answer I could find to the above questions was that I should now become the student. They would tell me about their experience; they would teach me how to live in this town. They would write and write, and I would read and read. And I would be stupid, a hick teacher, a dim-wit from the ivory town, and only by their writing alone would they be able to set me straight. I would ask them: "What's a good supermarket and a cheap restaurant and how do you get there, and what neighborhoods would you avoid?" And what happened? They wrote. They warned me away from certain restaurants and many supermarkets, and they laughed to find out one of those avoidable neighborhoods was my own. They tried to teach me how to find my way home while avoiding my own neighborhood, and they gave me advice about where to live next. And then they wrote some more, and I read some more, and eventually they felt comfortable enough with me to tease me about my hay-seed ignorance. As with almost any writing class, their stories began to unfold; but then, as with every class, their stories abruptly came to a halt at the end of the semester. As I think of them now, I suppose that I learned more than they did, but I will never know this for sure. They vanished back into the city, and my divided life still continues down its many-forked path.

And now a new semester. At Market University, I find that I am named in only two items out of seventeen in my student's law suit, his real grudge seeming to be against the permanent faculty. Meanwhile, back at Tech, I teach a class in communication skills. I was supposed to teach a different class, for which I was a last-minute substitution, but the first night the students arose en masse and declared that they thought it was really unfair that Kathy (whoever she was) was not teaching this class, and they walked out on me. To make everyone happy, I offered to switch classes with this Kathy, so now I teach what is essentially a speech class, something I've never really taught before.

Although my Tech students are more middle-class and certainly more white than they were on the downtown campus, each night is a lesson in diversity. I fill out my little forms on their cookie demonstrations and their sometimes meandering life stories. One young woman stands in front of us, telling us how her father used to disguise himself and follow her to the mall. One man speaks of the mystical link between Christ and a diet high in fiber. Another man explains the secret language of the used-car salesman. Then there is a woman who tells us cute stories about her son, beginning with his first cute stunt (which was, horribly enough, him toddling around the house with a huge cigar stuck in his mouth). Then the cute first words, the cute adolescent ordeals. With each cute story I grow more tense, thinking that any moment she is going to say, "—Little Gordie killed himself last week." I keep thinking she is setting us up for something awful, and so I am almost elated when she leaves the podium and little Gordie is still alive.

I don't know how any of these stories will end, and so, in my own way, I try to stay ready for anything. I don't know when the next student-I-will-never-forget will start spinning Humpty-Dumpty metaphors into a system of dread, or whether the men and women behind the mahogany desks will seek an out-of-court settlement with him or her. I don't know if the public safety officers will ever be stationed again outside my classroom or if they might be willing to take a bullet for me. My mother, now retired, recently told me that one of her former students honored her by writing that she was one of the reasons why he became a teacher. I doubt that such an honor will ever be mine, or whether I will know it if it is. Even so, I still carry the memory-become-dream of her one-room schoolhouse around with me.

Is this one-room school a bit of a romantic illusion? A bit of reactionary nostalgia? Does this dream signal the desire for the unities that only a rigid hegemony can keep in place? Is it just the dream of continuity in a profession that, every semester, feels a little bit more like channel surfing on cable television? Is it the simple artisan's dream of seeing some of the results of your work? I honestly don't know. The only thing I know for half-certain is where I keep this dream: if it's not in the trunk of my Chevy, then it's in my head as I continue to change my mind. I have taught now for fifteen years; in a few years more I may even have a permanent job or an office with my name on the door. Maybe I will someday have an old student show up and tell me the rest of his or her story. Maybe I will someday teach the son or daughter of a student I once taught. Perhaps I am kidding myself, but some days things seem to be working in that direction. I even have a few students this semester that I've taught before. They seem to be as shocked to see me as I am to see them, since my name is almost always listed in the course catalogue as "Staff." But I'm glad to see them. I want to carve their initials in the desk that I will one day have. I want to carve their names in all the weathered desks of my mother's one-room country school, where all the discontinuities of my continuing education began.

What Students Have Taught Me

Deanna L. Culbertson,
Douglas MacArthur State Technical College

After enduring a horrendous experience as a student teacher in a junior English classroom for sixteen weeks, I was not looking very forward to the career that I had worked so hard to prepare for for the past four years. I unenthusiastically went about the task of sending out résumés and filling out applications at every high school within a sixty-mile radius. Only one job for which I applied was not at a high school, but rather a technical college was looking for someone with a bachelor's degree in English to teach courses in developmental writing and reading. Reading that job description in the newspaper was the first I had heard of developmental education. After being hired for this position, I still did not really understand exactly what developmental education was. I was hired a couple of weeks before my first classes would begin, so during this time, I searched my college education books desperately for some type of description of and instruction in teaching developmental students, but none was to be found. I need not have worried, though, for it would be the developmental students themselves who would teach me not only the meaning of developmental education, but many other valuable lessons as well.

Finally, the first day of classes arrived, and I only knew that I would be teaching the basics; all the books, computer software, and materials I needed had been purchased for me, and all I had to do was assign each student to the appropriate book in the appropriate level, and I had it made—just sit back, grade tests, and answer questions.

"Good morning. My name is Mrs. Culbertson, and I'm so glad you are here. We have some forms to fill out first, and in order for me to get to know you a little better, I'd like for you to write your name on a piece of paper and then also write what you hope to get out of this class."

Well, that wasn't so bad; class was over. I had handed out all of the proper forms, including a syllabus which I explained in detail as the students stared bewilderingly at me; I had learned most of their names; and I had given them their first pretest. This developmental education was going to be a cinch!

During my first break, I got the chance to read the "What I Hope to Get Out of This Class" paragraphs that I had asked the students to write. I laughed as I read some of the typical answers: "To improve my writing and reading skills," "an A," and an occasional "I don't know." Then, I came across the two that nearly knocked me out of my chair: "To lern to read a bok," and "To betr mi redn skel." I quickly looked at the names at the tops of these papers. The first one belonged to Charlie, the student who had been in a wheelchair, and the second one to Fanny. I remembered from first period that they were the last ones to hand in their paragraphs. I went back to my room and frantically looked through all of the expensive materials that had been purchased for our new learning lab. Nothing would be adequate for these students. I would have to wing it until more materials could be ordered.

The next morning, I asked Charlie, Fanny, and another student from my afternoon class, Shedrick, if they could come at some other time so that we could all work together. We agreed upon 1:00 p.m. At just before one o'clock, construction had begun in the learning lab, which was not yet completely established. The instructor from the carpentry department was coming in and out bringing newly made computer desks for the lab, the communication electronics instructor was busily installing a telephone near my desk, and the electricity instructor, in an attempt to get the new computers up and running, was mumbling in frustration as he scanned the carpeted floor with a metal detector trying to locate the electrical outlets that were still in the floor from when the room had been used as a typing classroom. This chaos was still in full swing when my three reading students entered the room. I could see the fear, embarrassment, and confusion on their faces as they entered, so I rushed to meet them at the door and quickly hurried them to a small table at the back of the room where I began to attempt to determine at which level of reading each student was. Throughout the course of the next hour, they sounded short vowels and various consonants that they already knew. Quickly, I determined that Charlie was a little more advanced in reading than Fanny and Shedrick, and I gave him an activity to do while I worked a few more minutes with only Shedrick and Fanny. During this attempt, I discovered the severe speech problem, including stuttering, that Fanny had, so severe that I could barely make out some of the things she was trying to tell me. I then discovered the problems that Shedrick had that to this day, I still do not know how to classify. He told me of all the people who had "done him wrong" and how he planned to get back at them through various forms of explosions. At about this point the hammering, drilling, and conversation going on at the front of the lab had just become too much to try to teach over. Shaken by the conversation with Shedrick, frustrated about what I was going to do about Fanny's speech problem, but quite proud of myself for how quickly I had diagnosed these three students and begun to help them (and all on only my second day of teaching), I brought our class to an end. What happened next is a lesson that from which I have learned immensely and will never forget.

"Before we go, let me apologize for the noise and construction that has been going on during class today. Hopefully, it will be finished today, but just in case it is not, I will try to find another classroom in which we can meet for tomorrow. If the construction is still going on, I will leave you all a note on the door telling you where class will meet."

No one said anything for about ten seconds, when finally Charlie burst out in laughter, and said, "Mrs. Culbertson, we can't read!"

I tried to cover this humiliating error, but the deep shades of red inching up my face could not be concealed. Finally, I just had to laugh with them and change my instructions about the next day's class meeting, but inside I was devastated. I could not believe the error I had made, not just the error of telling illiterate students that I would leave them a note, but the error of thinking, subconsciously, that because they could not read that they were not perceptive; however, Charlie had humbled me. I would never underestimate students' perception and overestimate my ability to make a mistake again.

It has now been almost three years since that second day that I ever taught developmental students. Fanny has made some vast improvements in her speech and in her studies, although she still has a long way to go; Shedrick has completed almost all of his college studies, and he still tells me all of his strategies for revenge on those who have "done him wrong," but I have learned just to laugh, knowing that he is really harmless; and Charlie— well, although I had the great pleasure of awarding him with a certificate of achievement for completing his assigned books and learning to read, Charlie taught me more than I will ever teach him.

The Pleasures and Pains of Teaching: Is Anybody Listening?

Davie Davis, Central Missouri State University

As a writing lab instructor in an institution of higher learning, I find it impossible to leave my maternal tendencies home with the rest of the domestic clutter. Even though my own adolescent children scoff at my warnings to keep the clock radio at least three feet from their heads when they sleep, take their multivitamins daily and apply sunscreen on an hourly basis, I still naively expect that other people's children will listen to and heed my sage advice. For example, when I walked into the lab and discovered one of my student assistants munching her way through a chocolate bar, chips, and cola, I heard myself scolding, "Donna, what in the world are you doing?"

Her eyes widened in apprehension. "This is my lunch break. Isn't it all right to eat in here?"

"It's not all right to eat that kind of junk anywhere," I retorted, slamming my briefcase and books on the table for emphasis. "Don't you realize that all that fat and sugar and salt will raise your insulin levels, lower your blood sugar, clog your arteries, and depress your immune system, not to mention make your hair dull and your skin blotchy?"

Donna stared at the half-eaten candy bar in her hand and then replied ungratefully, "Gee, I guess I'm lucky to be alive, huh?"

I snorted and struck the classic hands-on-hips pose of indignant moms everywhere; however, Donna, unperturbed, had already turned back to her lethal feast. Trying to shake off any further concerns for her nutritional welfare, I made my way to a table of waiting students and was soon engrossed in my work, which is to help students who are having problems with their writing. Today I found the usual variety of unhappy clients, from a freshman irritated by the incomprehensible behavior of the apostrophe to a graduate student weary of wrestling with an unwieldy research proposal. As always, I tried to offer practical tips and advice which students could easily assimilate into their everyday writing rather than a lot of abstract grammatical rules.

"I'm still having trouble remembering the difference between *to* and *too*," confessed a non-traditional student with graying hair. He looked wistfully up at me from his paper, which was amply marked with his teacher's red ink. "I feel really dumb when I make such silly mistakes."

"Why don't you just write down the definitions of those words and tape the paper on your bathroom mirror?" I suggested. "That way, you can study them for a few moments every day while you shave."

He looked skeptical. "I'm not sure that will work for me."

As I gave his paper a final reading, I could feel my frustration level rising. All day, I tirelessly dispensed such suggestions, many times to students whom I would never see again. How did I know that any of them actually followed my recommendations, any more than this man intended to? Would the pretty blonde freshman review the apostrophe handouts I had given her, or would she carelessly leave them on a table in the student union, too busy chatting with her new friends to think any more about irregular plurals? Would the graduate student work on clarifying his muddled hypothesis, or would he obstinately leave it as it was, convinced that the middle-aged writing lab lady probably just didn't understand aviation technology anyway? Like my own children, who insisted on getting sunburns, library fines, colds, bug bites and flat tires despite my detailed instructions on how to avoid these catastrophes, did most of my writing lab students simply shrug off my helpful hints and advice once they escaped my vigilant eye? Unbeknownst to me, did they stubbornly wallow in comma confusion and rhetorical uncertainty for the rest of their college careers?

These uncomfortable thoughts were still crowding my mind as I greeted Natasha, an African-American social work major whom I had not seen since last spring. Obviously, her wardrobe of oversized overalls and tee-shirts hadn't changed, but then, neither had the congenial grin and bright brown eyes under the baseball cap. I felt certain that, despite the somewhat scruffy exterior, Natasha would make a wonderful social worker, but I knew that several of her professors had given her harsh warnings about her writing deficiencies.

"First writing assignment of the term," she announced ceremoniously, flinging her paper onto the table.

"Ten pages! Looks like you've been busy," I observed, as I settled in for some hard work. But as I began reading, it slowly dawned on me that this paper did not contain Natasha's usual number of errors. In fact, compared to her previous efforts, the writing seemed surprisingly complex and sophisticated. Halfway through our session, I couldn't help stopping to comment on her improvement.

"Nat, this paper is really super. How in the world did you make so much progress over the summer?"

Natasha smiled happily. "I just did exactly what you told me, Mrs. Davis."

I stared blankly at her. "I told you how to do this?"

"Sure, don't you remember?" she replied, and then, sitting up very straight, she gave a solemn recitation of my words from months ago. "You said I should go to the library every day over summer break and read articles by authors in my field. You said if I read enough, and studied enough, I could gradually absorb their writing style, just like a person who listens to music will find certain tunes running through his head."

Slowly last spring's conversation emerged from the murky depths of my memory. "Yes, that was a theory I picked up in a linguistics book," I said slowly. "I've told dozens of students to work on their writing through intensive reading." Then I blurted without thinking, "But none of them ever did it. I never expected that you would actually do it either!"

She leaned back and laughed. "Well, I did. And my teachers think I had a brain transplant or something."

I was so astounded by Natasha's revelation that I could barely concentrate on the remainder of her paper. I kept imagining her going faithfully to the library on the hot summer days, slowly but determinedly making her way through hundreds of pages of social work literature, all the while drawing hope and encouragement from a brief bit of advice that I had already forgotten. As we said our goodbyes, I began to wonder: How could I be so sure that all those other students hadn't done what Natasha had?

"Do you really think my skin is blotchy?"

I turned to see Donna standing behind me, hands raised to her face and eyes filled with worry. "No, I think you have beautiful skin," I assured her; then, seeing her relieved expression, I hastily added, "But it won't stay beautiful unless you get enough vitamins. Okay?"

She nodded. "I got out of class late and was in a hurry, so I just grabbed some stuff out of the vending machine. I'll do better tomorrow, I promise." To my amazement, she hugged me briefly before grabbing her backpack and skipping out the door.

Later that afternoon, as I walked down the leaf-strewn sidewalk to the parking lot, it seemed that the autumn sunshine was a little warmer, perhaps even a little brighter, than usual. I was trying to remember if the sunscreen in my medicine cabinet had expired when a voice behind me said, "I decided to keep that paper on my dashboard instead."

I looked around to see the gentle, gray-haired non-traditional student who had been in the lab earlier. He smiled and help up a piece of notebook paper. "I thought I could just as well study my *to* and *too* while I'm stopped at traffic lights as at the bathroom mirror. Besides," and her he paused, raising one hand to his neatly trimmed beard, "I don't shave much."

My mouth dropped a little. Then I joined him in a laugh as we headed toward our cars.

In Another Country:
What My Students Have Taught Me
Sally Griffith, Atlantic Community College

The community college where I teach is my favorite foreign country. I don't go for the scenery or the architecture or, heaven knows, the cuisine. I go, as I do to all foreign places, hoping to get glimpses into the natives' lives. I get on those big jets and roam stone alleys straight out of the glossy pages of *The National Geographic,* hoping for glimpses through open windows. I swoon when a homemade rocket, part of some pagan ritual, streaks into the sky after a bow from the sender to my daughter. But there's the hitch—unknowable. Glimpseable, but unknowable. It has gradually dawned on me that to know another culture I have only to walk into my classrooms, particularly those labeled developmental, where the students are free to write about themselves and generally unsophisticated enough actually to do so. They have given me another country, a country that was always right there under my nose. They have given me this with such detail and such depth that I can feel it. It gets into my pores and under my fingernails.

This country I have gradually learned to know is, of course, in the same county I live in. Its inhabitants, like me, are predominantly white and female. We all look middle-class, and that is how we all doubtlessly would describe ourselves. All deceptive. I leave behind me a trail of modest worldly gains, made possible by circumstances that made achievement easy. My students, on the other hand, are typically victims in almost every area of life, and they still persist, persisting with values that generally put the world of success to shame.

My students live in what is essentially a third-world country. They have little money and therefore few choices. They have been in and out of emergency rooms, but few ever visit a doctor or a dentist. They have been to a lot of funerals; everyone knows somebody who was murdered, somebody killed in an automobile crash, somebody who committed suicide. They work long hours at minimum wage, minimum satisfaction, jobs just to keep their wretched cars running, cars they occasionally live in. They have survived child abuse of every kind. They have been humiliated in school. They are surrounded by violence—violence is the normal way of doing things. They know about divorce and alcoholism and drug abuse from the inside, from inside their own families. Prostitutes walk their streets.

Right now I have a stack of research papers on my desk. Here are the titles: Incest, Child Sexual Abuse, The Effect of Divorce on Children, The Effects of Maternal Smoking on the Fetus, Gang Warfare, Suicide, Drug Abuse, Domestic Violence: Its Effect on Women, Guns and Drugs, Attention Deficit Disorder, Down's Syndrome, Contraceptives, Kids and Guns, Divorce, The Medical Effects of Alcoholism, Domestic Violence, Alcoholism: How It Affects the Family, Homelessness, Handguns. These are the concerns that grip my students' lives. No wonder they're not preparing to be brain surgeons and rocket scientists.

It took my breath away when the comparison first came to me, but the culture my students emerge from has much in common with the Mundugumore, one of the primitive peoples who live and breathe in Margaret Mead's *Sex and Temperament*. The Mundugumore tend their babies and children with the absolute minimum of contact necessary for survival and have a relationship system that pits almost everyone, beginning with husbands and wives, against everyone else. Mundugumore society is brutish, isolating and violent.

How would Mead describe my students' world? They typically come from single-parent households, and that one adult works full time, away from home, with a long commute. Further, like the Mundugumore, these households exist in isolation, with no network of nearby kin, no village to raise the child. When I look at a class of students, I am looking at young adults who spent their childhoods in car seats, in various day cares, eating fast food, watching television alone or with a stressed-out parent trying simultaneously to make it up to the kid and have some kind of decent life for herself. With no help. Music lessons? Reading together? Developing skills? Feeling treasured and encouraged? Like the Mundugumore, our society is set up so that, for the bottom half, these things are virtually impossible.

My students should be basket cases, and much of their cohort is. We have the national statistics to prove it. But here they are in my classroom, incredibly generous of spirit. Nobody sneezes without a chorus of "God bless you." When a classmate does well, they break into applause. When someone needs assistance, they sacrifice their own performance to help. They hold open doors for perfectly healthy people at the other end of the corridor. They create little communities in a hostile world.

My students, of course, do not have the knowledge and skills and habits they need to be successful in the country I live in. Nor do they have their tribe's treasury of knowledge—we don't sit around campfires transmitting ancient wisdom, and, heaven knows, television is no substitute. My students have spent twelve years dozing in class and often in the principal's office.

One rogue reported that he had forty-five days detention still to do when he graduated from high school.

When I look at elementary and high school through my students' eyes, they are different places than I remember. One of my developmental students recently wrote about his second-grade world. The second-graders (seven years old—the age at which Norweigan children begin school) were tested, and then he and his parents were summoned to a room full of big people to be told that he was gifted. Gifted! Nobody in his family had ever even graduated from high school, and now they had this *wunderkind* in their midst. His grandparents gave a party in his honor. Even the concrete looked different to him, a gifted person, as he walked to school. Six months later he and his parents were once again summoned to that room full of big people. They were told that a mistake had been made. (I would bet the farm that no one said, "We made a mistake" or "I made a mistake.") They were told that he was Learning Disabled. Six months later, in a repeat performance, they were told that he was average.

This child's world crashed around him. It has taken ten years to glue the pieces back together, and the joints still ache. What this remarkable young man is doing in college is painstakingly, step by step, working his way to be an elementary guidance counselor, a person who will see to it that what happened to him doesn't happen to other kids. He is a hero.

Here are three more of the many, everyday, community college heroes:

- A mother of three, now a single parent, working full-time, going to college full-time studying to be a teacher of mentally handicapped children, children like her own Down's Syndrome son, whom she writes about lovingly and proudly.

- As a child, this student was humiliated by her father, who made her wait on his girlfriends and beat her with a belt, buckle end. She and her husband raise their own four children and also foster children. She can't walk by a child in need.

- A radiant young woman, labeled Learning Disabled, teased and tormented by other children and constantly told by teachers that she would never amount to anything. She was a Playboy bunny until the night a thug worked over her face with a tire iron. Now she's a culinary student, while caring for her mother, an Alzheimer's patient. I have Christmas tree ornaments they made together.

What could be more amazing than to come out of a Mundugumore background and to bloom so sweetly? My students' country does not show up on the charts, nor is it seen by commentators. But I have been there. Henry David Thoreau once wrote that he had traveled widely in Concord. Now, I have traveled widely in Atlantic County.

Practical and Spiritual Advice for New Developmental Teachers

Jeremy W. Heist,
Chaffey College and Mt. San Antonio College

Your first developmental teaching assignment can be thoroughly successful, and you can have lots of fun in your classes, if you can just begin with the right attitudes, relax, and then set up a simple and regular classroom routine that embodies effective teaching principles.

The good news is: you already know far more about this course's subject matter than you will ever have time to teach, so you have no reason to "bone up" for this teaching assignment (except to get familiar with the textbook you will use), or to feel anxious about your own knowledge of the subject; at this fundamental level, your students surely need every bit of the information and skill that you will teach in this course, and most of them will see readily the relevance and usefulness of everything you're teaching them; so, all you need to do to teach a totally valuable lesson is to find out how your students would handle any routine verbal task, and then show them how to do differently anything that you, or anyone with your level of training and experience, would find faulty in their responses.

The bad news is: many of your students will have terribly low confidence in their ability to acquire verbal skills, and their anxiety may cause them to act bored, gloomy, tormented, or hostile; also, in a typical class, even students who have solid verbal skills and self-confidence may surprise you by their ignorance of academic survival necessities such as attending class, doing assigned tasks, meeting deadlines, taking notes, and following assignment specifications of length, topic, etc. You may encounter many students who have been passed through high school even when they ignored or failed most assignments, and some of these students will not believe, until it is too late, your warnings that they're now playing a new game with new rules.

No teaching method can make all your students sit in rapt delight through every meeting of your class and look forward to it as the high point of their week. Nothing can even guarantee that you will avoid the things that make some classes mostly depressing: earnest students who can't quite get it, troubled folks with chips on their shoulders, and those who would just obviously rather be any place other than school. But a few guidelines can keep your problems and frustrations at the lowest level you can hope for, until you develop all the specific teaching techniques that best fit your personality and situation. By following these guidelines, I think, you could at least free yourself from worrying that there might have been some major thing you should have done differently, and you can feel generally assured that what difficulties do arise are just those that are inevitable.

1. Approach Your Teaching with Appropriate Humility

Never allow yourself to feel condescending toward students simply because they are working with material that you consider elementary. Put yourself in your student's position by imagining yourself taking the equivalent of a developmental-level course in some subject you find intimidating— whether that's auto repair, computer science, Japanese, calculus, chemistry, accounting, or whatever. Picture yourself summoning the courage to break through your fears and mental blocks and go to school, when you could have been sitting at home watching TV, and then being confronted by a sneering instructor who can't believe there's anyone who doesn't already know the basic stuff of that course's material. To exhibit such condescension would be not only cruel and immoral, but also unproductive and distracting to your students, so by condescending you would become a mediocre teacher, and then everyone else could condescend to you! Consider too the possibility that some of your students may already have mastered many of the subjects that intimidate you, so as soon as they've learned what you know in your field, they'll be way ahead of you overall. If you have a fragile ego and must feel superior to someone, condescend to the people "out there" who don't know your material and *aren't* taking the class.

2. Don't Try to Be the "Star of the Show"

Teaching is not *exactly* show business, so find some way to set your ego aside, and just worry mainly about whether students are getting what they need to get, not about whether they think you're witty, cool, far-out, or rad, not about whether they'd like to have a mommy or daddy just like you, and not about whether they would view your class as entertainment on a par with MTV. No one expects you to infuse every moment in the classroom with some terribly "on," show-bizzy spark of improvisational creativity and/or profound wisdom. If you do a good, straightforward job of teaching your material, plenty of your students will appreciate you with a deep gratitude.

Again, imagine yourself taking one of those intimidating courses, and realizing that the instructor was preoccupied with being liked, and was making it his top priority to make the class entertaining. Wouldn't you say, "Hey, until I make sure that I can *pass* this course, I'm too tense to be entertained! Let's just get the job done, and we can yock it up after the final grades come in."

If you are a witty and/or likable person, your students will be amused and charmed, from time to time, when they don't have anything more important to do. But in any case, you can be useful, as long as you consistently give students skills and information that they lack.

Footnote on Textbook Use: Whether or not you adore the available textbooks, select one and make sure that your developmental class is linked quite closely to it. Your ego will often urge you to improvise your teaching materials from many sources, or—heaven forbid—to give students everything important in lecture form (so that everything they get will be just exactly right). But in my experience it seems to require a confident and classroom-savvy student to function well without having a single text at the core of the course; supplying all the same information on accumulated hand-outs just doesn't let as many of your students stay on track. Try to skip any textbook pages that flatly contradict your own ideas, but find a way to co-exist with the rest.

3. See Yourself as a Humble Servant

As a voluble person with an oversized ego, I find that my teaching goes best by far if I think of myself not as an oracle or sage but as something more like a waiter in a restaurant. As such, it is my job to serve whoever shows up at my tables, and to maintain a friendly and helpful posture, considering it at least somewhat my own loss if my customers are uncomfortable, and maintaining a dignified posture even as I work hard to serve their needs, not to force my choices on them.

This self-image is particularly comfortable for me when the most difficult situations arise. Just as the waiter must sometimes have the bouncer bounce a drunk, or must report a stolen credit card, so a teacher must get rid of students who can't stop conversing or otherwise disrupting a class, and must shock others by pointing out high-schoolish study habits that just won't work any more. In the posture of the humble servant, I find that these "cop's jobs" can be carried out with a minimum of confrontation, and that a surprising number of problem students can change their habits on the spot if approached humbly with facts and policies rather than by an unequivocally menacing and righteous figure of authority.

4. Steal Your First Syllabus, and Modify It Later

At most schools, departmental course descriptions will specify certain items that your course must cover, and you can obtain copies of syllabi that previous teachers have used for the course in question. Try to get hold of a sample syllabus involving the same textbook(s) and the same number of meetings per week that you will have, and for your first go-round just adapt that to the current calendar; or else, get a sample syllabus for the course when it meets just once a week, and divide the weekly content up over the days you're scheduled to teach. Then, keep a few weeks ahead of the class, actually doing all exercises and assignments, and modify the syllabus for up-coming weeks if you feel you need to.

5. *Emphasize and Repeat a Finite Number of Vital Points*

If possible, work through the whole course quickly before the term starts, and try to identify *a modest number* of important points that you can emphasize repeatedly throughout the course. Ask yourself: What five or ten skills that could be acquired, or behavioral changes that could be effected, would yield the most far-reaching and seminal benefits to a student's verbal skills? You may touch on dozens of separate "do's" and "don'ts," etc., in the course of the term, but you should have a handful of essential themes that you keep coming back to, repetitiously. Remember, what might seem excessively redundant to an expert can often be reassuring, as well as helpful, to a beginner: If the student understood the point on its first time around, he/she will get a sense of achievement and confidence, and a deserved vacation from mastering new material, when that point comes around again; those who didn't get it the first time can get another shot, perhaps this time with some additional help from fellow students who've gotten it "down cold" (see section below on Collaborative Learning).

Ideally, you want to find principles that will continue to lead the student onward and upward, "gifts that keep on giving," like perhaps in a writing course: the basic concept of support as giving the reader the sense of *seeing*, of being shown in pictures rather than told in words, what the writer has asserted; or specific techniques for making supporting details seem more solid and real by making them appeal to the senses; or, of course, the basic "process" concept of writing as a series of discrete steps and revisions, in which it's perfectly OK to pursue one objective at a time, rather than trying to get everything right at once.

But the most important point is that, especially at the Developmental level, and very possibly in all teaching, it is better to err on the side of teaching a bit too little material and teaching it indelibly, rather than skimming over a lot of stuff that nobody quite gets, and then just being able to "say you've been there."

6. *Teach Skills Students Will Be Rewarded Outside Class for Learning*

Generally speaking, if I have to weed out a lot of potentially useful material from my course plan, I use two different criteria for deciding what to keep: (1) I try to steer students away from whatever types of verbal behavior might get them into the most trouble—i.e. might lead employers, other teachers, or anybody with the most common prejudices or phobias about language use, to dismiss the student as illiterate, incompetent or stupid; and (2) I also try to calculate which new skills a student will have the most fun with, or will bring the student most ego satisfaction—on the theory that acquiring these skills may inspire the student to keep acquiring further skills, in a life-long process of learning.

7. Don't Use Your Own Most Recent Teachers as Models

If your most recent teaching models have been graduate-level university teachers, you probably can't base your classroom techniques very much on their examples.

First of all, there are regrettably many high-level teachers who have never had to master any sound pedagogical methods, because their students have mostly been talented, trained, and specialized enough that courses can run on automatic pilot if the teacher simply orders some books, makes a schedule, and writes out a few essay assignments. Advanced students can be expected to know all the classroom routines, and to "fill in the blanks" of standard academic operating procedure with the data from the reading list at hand. Professors who have taught only at this level are the academic equivalent of those basketball coaches who can recruit "blue chip" super-athletes and conduct practices simply by tossing out a basketball and letting the kids start a playground-style scrimmage. Even teachers who are deficient by these lax standards are seldom exposed or confronted, because the more advanced the level, the easier it is to blame failures on student preparation for that level: "By the time they get to my class, they're supposed to know (whatever)!"

Thus, many professors do not appear to have ever undertaken the fundamental teaching task of preparing a lesson for a class, i.e. determining what the students need to "get," and what will be the quickest and surest way to make sure that they get it. Instead, these professors apparently prepare as they would if they were taking, rather than teaching, the class: they read, or look over, the assigned material, and come into class prepared to offer their off-the-cuff thoughts and responses. This approach can be rationalized and justified as "spontaneous" and "natural," rather than "regimented" and "rigid," and the teacher can claim that he's offering his students a shortcut to wisdom and sophistication by showing them how a highly cultivated man like himself reacts instinctively to certain intellectual stimuli. This approach can easily ignore important fundamental points as "too obvious," instead favoring esoteric afterthoughts, nuances, and unanswered questions over "first things first" emphases; and it tends to sacrifice organization for randomness glorified as spontaneity.

8. Use Drills and Comprehension Checks Promptly and Repeatedly

Never go more than about five minutes, if possible, without giving the student something to do with the information you are presenting: (1) Explain a point, by yourself, using the blackboard; (2) show students where in the text the same point is covered, if it is; (3) get students to apply the point to textbook exercises, or to problems you make up and throw at them; (4) explain where students have exhibited misunderstandings in applying these points; and then (5) try some new exercises. If students seem to welcome a challenge, sometimes it can be effective to let them try some exercises before you state the point, and thereby fuel their appetite for understanding the concept before you've even brought it up.

Do not be afraid to use exercises with recurring or predictable patterns when students are practicing new concepts. Again, put yourself in the student's place (imagining a course in some field intimidating to you): when the material is *not* "old hat," the student is normally relieved and grateful to practice it in a familiar and even repetitious format, especially if you have required more than five minutes or so of stressful, more "free-form," mental concentration while you were presenting the basic points of the lesson.

9. Make the Quicker Students Help You Teach

If you have overqualified students for whom everything seems a bit too easy, you do not have to abandon them to boredom. The answer I have found is to articulate early the principle that, as soon as anyone fully grasps a point, that person essentially changes jobs, from student to teacher. In other words, you begin teaching students from the first day of the semester that grasping or "getting" the point is only the first of two steps: the second step is figuring out how to pass the idea along to any of the varied people one might ever meet who have not yet grasped it.

In teaching the material yourself, you will have realized that this second step is virtually infinite in scope, and no student will exhaust its possibilities. (If anyone comes close, get him/her a Student Aide job in the campus learning center/tutorial lab.) Of course, there is much more than "busy work" involved in teaching this principle: apparently all the proselytizing religions whose missionaries knock on our doors have discovered that an idea becomes most solidly ingrained in a person only when that person sets out to transmit it, not merely to prove that he himself has grasped it.

10. Change the Pace and Vary Activities in the Classroom

In any class, but especially at the Developmental level, where attention spans may be shorter and frustration levels lower, it is important to vary the shape and format of activities in a single class meeting. I sometimes think of a class by analogy to a nighttime TV talk show, on which a producer might schedule an actor, a singer, and an author, but not three in a row of any one kind. However you picture the situation, you want to create a sense of pattern that depends on each segment simply feeling distinct from the last. Even in a fifty- or seventy-five-minute period, make sure that you do at least two, and preferably several, different types of work—just so that everyone in the class will be jolted into motion, and forced to "shift gears," thereby combatting inertia and boredom. Conceivably a group of Ph.D. candidates in a seminar could sit for two hours and hammer away at the same task—but even there, I suspect, their productivity and creativity would improve if the form of their activities could be varied. With Developmental students, you will learn quickly that the best-planned, most inherently interesting lesson can begin to fail if it drags on too long without the kind of superficial format variation that signals a new beginning.

11. Use Collaborative Learning Groups

I was a late and reluctant convert to Collaborative Learning—the process of dividing classes into groups of three or four students to work on group tasks for segments of twenty to forty minutes—but today I would dread the prospect of teaching without it, especially at the Developmental level.

The benefits of using Collaborative Learning groups include the following: (1) anxious students will relax somewhat, and begin to work on course tasks without worrying so much about pleasing the teacher, or maintaining an image toward the larger group of students; (2) shy students who won't speak much in the larger class often participate enthusiastically in groups; (3) the more advanced students can become champions or heroes, of a sort, like jocks on the athletic fields, when they do more than their share of the work on a successful graded group task—and thus, more students gravitate toward "the brain" as a role model; (4) many students will admit to their peers but not to the teacher that they have missed or forgotten some entire concept that they know has been emphasized—and often their peers can help them catch up without exposing what they missed; (5) group work is probably the ultimate "change of pace" available for varying the texture and rhythm of classroom tasks, in that it replaces the solitude of the individual in his/her wing-desk with the camaraderie of the team enterprise; and (6) Collaborative Learning groups provide, incidentally, a wonderful device for the teacher to use—especially at the beginning of the semester—for making friends with students, or at least getting students to perceive the teacher as a potentially likable human being. First, the mere fact that in groups students can get away from the teacher for a while seems to free them somehow to feel friendly faster, even if the teacher spends the time grading quizzes or writing new material on the blackboard. Then, too, the teacher can circulate among groups, pulling up a chair and listening in, and can act casual and personable, or even goof around a bit, thus relaxing many students. Above all, if you give students a graded group task, and you offer to chip in with some limited amount of coaching, you will usually get all the groups yelling at you to come over and help *them*, and many students then begin to see your knowledge as an asset valuable to them, rather than as a bottomless pool of unanswerable questions with which you plan to torment them throughout eternity.

12. Direct Most Tasks Toward Upcoming Graded Work

Do not suppose that it is somehow crass if almost everything that you do in class is directly relevant to some graded task that students will be doing shortly. Teachers tend to quote with scorn the student's eternal query, "Will this be on the test?" But it is arrogant absurdity to pretend that any classroom full of students, especially beginners, should be motivated purely by the desire to commune with their teacher about the mysteries of life, language, or literature. Remember that most of your students have complex lives and have to prioritize their tasks and obligations: they have other classes, sometimes as many as five or six that they are trying to carry, often a job or multiple jobs, families that need attention, and houses that need repairs—not to mention personal crises, like medical problems, deaths in the family, divorces, children in trouble, ex-spouses stalking them, drive-by shootings on their street, etc. If you want them to allocate their time and concentrate on your lesson, it's only reasonable that you give them a reason to do so, and the obvious reason is that without the information you are presenting, they will probably get a lower grade on some upcoming piece of work.

If possible, set up Developmental classes with a great many separate pieces of graded work, including short, mostly simple quizzes at the end of almost every meeting. Then let a certain number of the lowest grades, in each category of graded work, be discarded, so that it is impossible to ruin one's grade without establishing a consistent pattern of failure, but so that the most conscientious students, who always take their best shot at every task, will normally get a grade-boost bonus for their consistency. Ending classes with a quiz is very helpful in keeping students focused and alert (rather than leaning toward the exits with their minds already out in the parking lot) until the class is completed.

Above all, stay relaxed, and insist on enjoying your teaching—as these principles can allow you to do, once you understand that they assure you of making a useful contribution whenever you teach.

Putting Myself in Jeopardy

Robert Hughes, Harry S. Truman College

This is my fatal fantasy: I am standing in front of my community college English as a Second Language writing class, but I am not myself; I am Alex Trebek, host of the hit TV quiz show *Jeopardy*. I am charismatic, brilliant, good-natured and, most of all, in charge. I conduct the class with all the speed and sparkle of an auctioneer with terrific stuff to sell. The students feel this. My questions challenge them. My manner inspires them. Bells ring, buzzers buzz, things move at a bracing clip. They grow in knowledge and fluency and admiration of me, their handsome host.

The trouble is, my students, most of them elderly and from the former Soviet Union, want none of this. Their ideal would be one of those Sunday morning fishing shows, slow-moving, easy on the eye and low on the stress monitor, one where the host glides leisurely down the Nippersink River in boots and flannel shirt discussing bait and reels while the viewer takes in the scenery. Their attitude is, "We've had enough challenges already, thank you, in having uprooted ourselves from everything we know and attempting to live in this prosperous but strangely competitive land. Let's just coast for a while, OK?"

What triggers their attitude is a phenomenon I think of as Vocabulary Panic. This show-stopping syndrome grips my students frequently, especially when they pick up on the fact that I expect things to move along at a lively rate. When Vocabulary Panic takes hold, no progress can be made until everybody knows the precise spelling, denotation and connotation of every word I've used. A bugle call for stall tactics is blown, and I am left outflanked, helpless, stupefied.

This clash of fantasy scenarios creates a variety of interesting television but neither of the shows we want.

Monday Night Football. By far the most successful stall tactic is the Page Number Offensive. Before any mind-fogging vocabulary has been thrown at them, before any class pace has been established, I am hit with a preemptive strike.

I waltz into the classroom. We exchange cheerful greetings. I ask them to turn to page 148 in our textbook. The smiles are replaced by looks of hopeless confusion. Then one student turns to another and says, audibly and despairingly, "What page?" The maneuver is repeated down the row like "the wave" in the stands on *Monday Night Football.* The wave undulates back and forth and around and around the room as I stand in front of them repeating "page 148" like a zombie. But nothing can stop the wave. It has a life of its own and ends only when it has run itself out. To an insecure opponent, as I normally am, the wave is a debilitating play, and I fail to recover the initiative.

The most breathtaking instance of the Page Number Offensive that I have ever witnessed occurred one day twenty minutes after class had begun. A student in the back row failed to get a wave going at the start of the class. So after we had been working on an exercise in our text for fifteen minutes or so, she struck again. I laid myself open and said, "OK, class, let's turn the page and continue." Then she hit and hit hard: "Same book, teacher?"

Daytime Talk Show. By this I certainly do not mean Oprah, who runs a tight ship and whom I strive vainly to emulate. No, my class often resembles one of the new talk shows run by an inexperienced host who lets the audience throttle the topic any way they please. This host dashes from one end of the set to the other trying to control people as they opine on such topics as "Husbands who leave towels on the floor" or "Mothers who date their daughter's best friend's cousins."

The top-rated topic of my class is, "Words that teachers use to drive their students crazy." It doesn't matter what I think the topic for the day is— paragraph development, rewriting, subordination, transitions—the actual topic simmers in their heads until some word I use brings it to a rolling boil. I might write on the board some such sentence as, "Though John's horse walks slowly, his sister's horse gallops." I've hardly put the chalk down before I know it's all over for me. "Gallop?" someone says out loud to no one in particular. "Gallop? What is gallop?" And the debate is on. Dictionary pages fly fast and furiously. Students spin in every direction discussing the ins and outs of the controversial word. Meanwhile, back at the front of the room, I am bounding like Secretariat back and forth, whinnying and snorting my heart out. But no one is looking at me.

Now not every student is a victim of Vocabulary Panic. Some students know the word in question, but enjoy the entertaining break. Some are perfectionists who figure out quickly what the word means from context but won't be happy until they've looked it up and had it confirmed by others. But the truly panic-stricken go deaf when they hear an unfamiliar word. In the grip of an obsession, they take over the class until they've wrestled the word to the floor.

Stand-up Comedy.   Nothing brings out their fears like my attempts at humor. When a genial TV quiz show host breaks his routine to tell a joke, even a lame one, it isn't met with confusion, embarrassment, insincere laughter, and pity. But this is how my jokes are routinely greeted, even my finest one about Clark Kent, the top of the Sears Tower, a bartender, and a farmer named Clovis. Believing in this joke with a fanatic's fervor, I tell it and retell it every year, hoping that by antecedent planning, explanations, acting out, and *actual dictionary use*, this masterpiece will leave them wheezing at their desks in delight and feeling pleased with their grasp of English.

But by the time Clovis has hit the pavement and the bartender says, "Superman, you can really be a creep sometimes," the joke has been chopped into so many pieces that it no longer resembles a joke so much as a cross-word puzzle read aloud, haltingly. The students must inwardly sigh in relief, for the struggle to laugh politely while pretending to understand gibberish takes a lot out of a person. Getting back to normal tedium is, for them, a positive joy.

Situation Comedy.   The essence of effective pacing for both the quiz show host and the teacher is readiness. So once when an elderly student was confused by my too-rapid speech and my horrid handwriting on the blackboard, I was ready for her to try to improve the situation for herself. I was ready for her to move to the front row and adjust her desk. I was ready for some squinting and pointing and frowning. I was ready for her to pull her dictionary out of her bookbag with a flourish and scowl into it. I was ready for some theatrical putting on and taking off of glasses and shuffling of notes and shaking of the head.

But I wasn't ready for the binoculars. I wasn't ready for a look of stunned exasperation, followed by the production of a pair of field glasses and the slow scanning, from the front row, of my sentence, "Alice likes cheeseburgers." I wasn't ready for the class to dissolve into tears of laughter as I flailed about trying to re-choreograph my little instructional song and dance and wished classes, like TV shows, had commercial breaks.

It's easy to see why new, unfamiliar words strike fear in immigrant students. Words signify everything that blocks them from a full life in their new country. And I know it must be especially strenuous for an older student, who hasn't been in a class in years, to keep up with a hyperkinetic quiz show host of a teacher. However, unless I move abroad and learn a foreign language while leaving most of my property, part of my family, and all sense of social position behind, I'm sure I can never fully appreciate what they face.

But I do have an inkling. Just before the birth of my first child, I once visited briefly the foreign land and threatening vocabulary of a Lamaze childbirth class. The teacher was terrific and moved along at the respectable clip of the *Nightly News* if not exactly the dazzling speed of *Jeopardy*. But I had questions, so one night I brought up some of the issues that troubled me. *Exactly* how many contractions should there be before you think of racing to the hospital? *Exactly* how much time should elapse between contractions? What, exactly, *is* a contraction? How can it be distinguished from a false contraction, exactly? As my cross-examination started to veer into Perry Mason land, she said, "Excuse me, sir. But let me make a guess. Are you a teacher?"

So there I was. Faced with an issue that was, for me, borderline terrifying, I too had gone on the defensive and stopped the class dead. And as my wife tried to disappear into the floor, I realized there wasn't going to be any supporting "wave"; no "offensive" was about to be launched. I was on my own.

I keep this little episode in my mind as I, the smooth *Jeopardy* host, stand in front of my class and strive to make the show go my way. And these days when my students start to look overwhelmed, I sometimes scrap Double Jeopardy for the day, tie on a fly, cast out a line, and try to relax with them on the Nippersink for a while.

After all, Alex Trebek could handle that.

The Tortoise and the Snare, or The Comic Side of Teaching

Laurie Kaiser, Gulf Coast Community College

When I was a newspaper reporter covering education, I encountered a controversial superintendent of schools who insisted upon including "sense of humor" in every job description within his school system. It became a standing joke. In response to critics, the man replied, "I'm not looking for a comedian. I'm looking for someone who has the ability to keep things in perspective." Now that I am a a a teacher, I know what he knows: A sense of humor arms one for survival in education.

Nowhere but here in developmental education is a sense of humor so important to survival. Like other developmental teachers, I keep waiting for a miracle to occur. I continually remind myself of the titles of books I've read about teaching. They speak of *small* victories, shining *moments*, and compromise. In teaching preparatory English at a small two-year college in an economically depressed community in the Florida Panhandle, I have experienced small victories, but also colossal defeats; shining moments, as well as dismal days—and, of course, a great deal of compromise. I admit this freely. In fact, I've told my department head that I doubt my ability to reach students at this level. She says it isn't my failing. Then whose is it? I wonder. I teach Fundamentals of Composition, a course in which the expected success rate department-wide is 50 percent. To move beyond this rate seems a herculean task, yet this is my goal. I begin the semester with the resolve of Hercules and wind up the semester with the frustration of Sisyphus. Focusing on the comic side of teaching helps me to persist.

John Steinbeck's description of a tortoise negotiating an embankment comes to mind. Taken from *The Grapes of Wrath*, the piece describes in painful detail the difficulties the plodding land turtle encounters in trying to climb a roadside embankment. In the end, the tortoise triumphs. We discuss this excerpt in the developmental composition class when we study descriptive writing. Most students dismiss the piece as boring, failing to see the tortoise as a metaphor for the Oklahoma farmer during the Depression—or indeed anyone who faces obstacles. One student who did make the connection said she also saw humor in Steinbeck's description of the land turtle's struggles. Theresa summed up the piece by saying, "If you can look up, you can get up."

I feel like that tortoise sometimes, "boosting and dragging his shell along." I teach in Panama City, often referred to as the "Redneck Riviera" and Spring Break capital of the United States. The median household income among the city's 35,000 residents is about $25,500, according to the county Chamber of Commerce. The federal government classifies this area as economically depressed for the purpose of forgiving student loans to teachers. Education here is lacking. According to a recent report from the Florida Department of Education, four out of ten Florida college and university freshmen aren't ready for college-level reading, writing, and math. Only 42 percent of those entering community college are prepared for college-level work, hence the need for developmental courses. Roughly 40 percent of all Florida high school freshmen don't make it out of high school.

It is difficult to teach English in a place where the language is often abused. A sign before a bridge signal warns, "Load to high when flashing." A local shopping center's billboard boasts prices "lower then the competition." The marquee outside a topless bar reads, "It's a business doing plesure with you." There is Laura's Resturant [*sic*] and Gleen's Bar-B-Que. (Actually, the name is "Glenn's," but the sign says "Gleen's" on one side.) People here "wonder" through the park, rather than "wander." Once when I asked students to identify the second person plural, they said earnestly, "Y'all." If a teacher upholding commonly accepted standards of higher education doesn't have a sense of humor here, he or she will certainly fold. Laughter is close to tears.

Two years ago, during my first year of teaching, I worked with a male student who routinely disrupted class by making statements with sexual undertones. He directed these remarks most often at female students and sometimes at me. During a particularly hectic peer-editing workshop reorganization, I hastily said, "John, will you do my paper?" (I, too, participate in writing workshops.) "I'd love to do you," he replied, with the emphasis on "do." I pulled him aside after class to tell him that sexual innuendo would not be tolerated in my class. He looked at me blankly and said, "Yes," before departing. Later in the week, I came upon this entry in his journal: "I'm sorry I disrupted the class. I didn't know what 'in you window' meant. I never heard that term before." I learned something: Choose words carefully and always offer synonyms for difficult words.

Also in one of my early composition classes, we had the good fortune to celebrate a student's wedding. Every paper the student wrote had something to do with the wedding. For the strategy of process analysis, she wrote about planning a wedding. For comparison/contrast, she discussed the merits of indoor versus outdoor weddings. For description, she offered a glowing word portrait of her fiance. Generally, I let students choose their own topics because I figure if they write about something they care about, the work will reflect a certain energy. This is not necessarily so. Consider this another lesson learned. Robin's narrative was the proverbial frosting on the (wedding) cake. Here is an excerpt from the account of her wedding day:

> Now it was time for my dad and I to go. The wind was blowing my veil around. As we walked down the isle I heard my grandmother say, "God Robin your goregious." When we reached the alter my dad gave me away to my husband to be, he was stuuning in his white tux with tails. The vest and bow tie was the perfect touch. We said our vows and the preacher announced us husband and wife. We walked down the isle and formed a recieving line to greet relatives and friends.

With some guilt I assigned an "F" to the essay, commenting that the unfortunate errors detracted seriously from the piece about her special day.

During teacher training at Brown University, we novices were taught that all students are motivated and that we as teachers simply need to find relevant material to tap this wellspring of motivation. Frankly, I'm still walking around with my divining rod. What is relevant to them beyond cars, sex, and MTV? They view writing as an archaic exercise. They don't see the importance of looking smart on paper because they can communicate orally. When they enter the classroom, they don't seem eager for self-improvement, but rather for entertainment. I have acquiesced to a degree by conducting what amount to dog and pony shows in my developmental classroom—from standing at the front of the room with jars of peanut butter and jelly, a sack of bread and a knife and asking students to tell me how to make a peanut butter and jelly sandwich to placing them in groups to work on writing an illustration paragraph on an adage, such as "A stitch in time saves nine." Still I look around the room and see disengaged students: young women, their eyes crossed, examining their hair for split ends and young men, their mouths agape in a yawn.

Some students pretend to hear me. They deserve nominations for Academy Awards. They feign attention by looking directly at me and at peers, by nodding and smiling, and then they do the opposite of whatever we agree is best for their writing. I recall a particular discussion about word choice, and more specifically, about avoiding clichés. I passed around a Gary Larson "Far Side" cartoon which illustrates the absurdity of clichés. The cartoon depicts a mother and son in a crowd. The boy is reaching out to touch a floating face. The mother tells her son, "Don't touch it, honey . . . it's just a face in the crowd." A few of the students laughed; others looked puzzled. At least one student, judging by the next essay she submitted, thought I said, "Use clichés in your writing." In her comparison/contrast essay about her first impression of a sales tax proposal and a later point of view, Becky wrote, "My first impression of the . . . sales tax and my later point of view were as different as night and day. As if someone yelled in my ear, 'Wake up and smell the coffee.'"

Perhaps I agonize over the students' progress, or lack thereof, more than they. At midterm and end of term, I am understandably concerned about their progress because they are about to take a standardized examination of grammar and writing. The questions race through my mind: Have I prepared them well enough to pass this exam? Do they recognize unnecessary shifts in verb tenses? Can they differentiate between a dependent and an independent clause? Can they recognize commonly confused and misused words? Can they fix run-ons, comma splices, and sentence fragments? Can they write a coherent paragraph? Do they have a clue? Last year, during a review for the midterm exam, I asked students if they had any questions about the material. Verb-tense inconsistencies, perhaps? No. Identifying a prepositional phrase? No. "Speak to me, please," I said. A hand went up. A question at last, I thought. "Yes, Billy." "Can we leave early if we finish the exam before the end of the period?" Just the week before, these students urged me not to give outside assignments because the fair was in town.

I want badly for them to succeed, but sometimes wonder how much they want to succeed. Approaching each new batch of papers with sincere hopes of good reading and signs of real progress, I am frequently disappointed. One of my students recently wrote a paper on teachers' "pet peas." He went on to detail not the fun and enjoyment you can receive from owning one of these darling little green vegetables, but instead discussed things that teachers dislike. Speaking of pet peeves, one of mine is students who don't read. Their mistakes in writing betray their lack of reading. I have read students essays describing "tyed eye" shirts, similarities and differences between two "amazement" parks, and directions on how to make barbecued ribs with cornbread and "collar" greens.

Like Steinbeck's tortoise, I continue to climb the embankment. A few students will climb it with me. Every semester, I hope more will try and will succeed. ("As the embankment grew steeper and steeper, the more frantic were the efforts of the land turtle.") With a sense of humor, we can get through the weed-choked path to higher ground. As one of the students who made it said, "If you can look up, you can get up."

Wings on Their Wheelchairs

Margaret Ann Maricle, Cuesta College

Alan's father was a widely respected attorney who had edited a national law review. Alan struggled his entire life with a learning disability. His father had issued judgments that had made history in legal circles. Alan found C's as difficult to achieve as counting the stars in the heavens. A's were inconceivable, but his father expected them. He refused to admit his son had a learning disability and didn't even realize Alan was taking developmental classes in college. For a lifetime Alan had lived in the shadow of this great man and fought constantly against his resulting self-doubt. Therefore, I wasn't surprised the day that Alan sat in my office and cried; I'd seen him through a number of bouts with discouragement.

"It's the last week before finals and here I am—still totally confused. I spent the last three hours in the library on just this assignment." He stabbed his pencil at the paper. "Anyone else could have done it in half an hour."

I acknowledged his frustration and noticed that he was having to fight back tears.

"I'm just so tired of having to work harder than everyone else because of my disability," he said. "Will it always be this difficult?"

I didn't know exactly how to respond because I've never been very good at confronting someone with painful reality. I tried to penetrate the dark glasses he had just put on so I could at least tender the truth with a little compassion.

"It will probably always be this hard, yes. At least academically," I added.

"I guess I've always known that. Yet something keeps me going. I'm not sure what, though." He hesitated and then sat up a little straighter. "But I do know one thing—I've gotten this far, and I'll be damned if something as easy as sentence combining is going to stop me now."

He closed his English book and stood up. "Thanks for listening," he said.

I'm the one who should have said, "Thank you," for Alan, like so many of my students, has taught me more than I could ever have taught him.

Several of my students have learning disabilities and physical challenges which, instead of limiting them, have actually propelled them to greater heights of success. Whether consciously or not, these individuals have regarded their disabilities as opportunities, not limitations. And by example I have learned a great deal from these students who seem to possess a unique strength that allows them to rise above their particular difficulties.

Mack is the student who first made me aware of this ability to surmount challenges. When he rolled into my class the first day, he exuded more confidence than one might expect of a person in a wheelchair. He was such a good-looking young man that many of the female students did a double take, and one admitted later to having a "crush" on him. I, too, was easily taken in by his charm. He came in every day with a smile on his face, contributed freely to class discussions, and joked easily with me and his classmates. He teased me unmercifully about my handwriting being worse than his chicken scratching, which resulted from his misshapen hands.

"At least I have an excuse," he quipped.

He never let me get away with being late, saying that if he could get to class on time in his outdated chair, then he had every right to expect me to be more prompt. He questioned everything but never asked for special treatment. After a while I forgot that he was at a physical disadvantage and one day asked him if he'd walk over to the door and turn off the lights.

"I'd be happy to, but would it be OK if I just rolled over there?" he asked.

For a moment I was embarrassed until I saw that amiable grin. And then I felt uplifted. I'd forgotten that he was in a wheelchair. I'd gone beyond his disability, as he had done and expected me to do.

Later I talked to him about the incident. I explained that I just thought of him as able to function like everyone else. He smiled and told me that was exactly what he wanted me to think. He said that he could not only function as well as everyone else, but sometimes even better.

I continued to watch Mack draw people to him with his effusive personality and positive attitude. He didn't know the word "can't," didn't know what it meant to give up.

During a class discussion one day Mack told us of an incident that infuriated me but gave me even greater respect for him. He had gone into a gift store to shop, and the owner came over and asked him to leave. When Mack asked why, the man told him that he didn't want Mack crashing into his merchandise with his chair and breaking things. Mack very politely replied that he was quite skillful in maneuvering himself but would gladly leave if that's what the owner needed. Mack felt no anger, just regret for the man's lack of understanding.

This optimism, remarkable in itself, is even more significant, when one realized that Mack once had normally functioning limbs. He had known the joy of running free on the beach, had felt the satisfaction of building something with his hands, and could trust his capacity for memory and clear thinking, until a motorcycle accident and an ensuing coma denied him physical freedom and caused him to have to relearn how to learn. But Mack got back up from this temporary grounding, and when he couldn't walk any more or ride his motorcycle as fast as he wanted to, he learned instead to fly. Mack found wings for his wheelchair and never touched the ground again unless he chose to. Mack's wings were his positive attitude, his refusal to give up in the face of the darkest storm cloud. I could learn from that, I who spend a lot of time looking down or looking back, but not nearly enough time looking up. Mack taught me the true meaning of optimism.

Shannon's figurative wheelchair was her epileptic disorder, which had plagued her for years, subjecting her to embarrassment and fear of a public seizure and causing her to doubt her ability to learn as easily as others. One day Shannon sat next to my desk and trembled as she described her seizure that morning. She shared her mortification that her male roommate had discovered her nude and convulsing in the shower. Her emotions were so volatile as we talked that she was unable to function without crying; her ability to think clearly was temporarily impaired. On top of everything else, she knew she wouldn't be able to attend her first class. I managed to convince Shannon to go to the health center and made her promise to talk to the nurse about her emotional concerns.

Shannon's greatest concern was the difficulty she faced in meeting all the demands of going to school, working, and supporting herself without becoming overly stressed, for it was often the stress that triggered a seizure. I watched Shannon struggle for the entire semester with these concerns, watched her juggle all her demands, and wanted desperately to help.

But what kept me from intervening was Shannon's zest for living. In spite of these problems, she had an excitement about life that I rarely see. She couldn't wait to come to my class, to attend other classes, to learn as much as she could. She was impatient to try out the things she learned, frequently coming in to tell me of a successful experience with a new reading technique or a time management plan. Shannon loved life, as tenuous as it might seem at times to her. She couldn't wait for the next experience, despite the knowledge that the experience might be a seizure. Many of us take life for granted, failing to see the budding trees in spring or the sunset that paints the sky purple and orange. Shannon lived for those occurrences and shared them with all who would listen. She had an insatiable curiosity that kept her looking forward to that next exciting moment in her life. That love for life gave Shannon wings, allowing her a perspective few of us have. I'm glad she shared this perspective with me, for her passion inspired me and helped me to revitalize my sometimes waning enthusiasm.

Jeff, on the other hand, didn't have that appreciation for life. He often walked around in a self-induced fog, fighting powerful negative messages whose source he didn't at first understand and couldn't articulate. Jeff found it difficult to concentrate, to focus, to understand even basic information at times. Many of his instructors found him annoying. He asked too many questions; he had no commitment; he was inconsistent. Yet I saw in Jeff a yearning to be free of this emotional limitation with which he struggled. I cannot begin to describe or define or even give it a psychological label, but I saw that Jeff was fighting against a terrible emotional foe, which sometimes left him debilitated.

So many times I heard what sounded like excuses from him. "I couldn't come to class . . . or get my paper done . . . or study for my test . . . because I just have these negative voices in my head."

At first I was impatient with him and reminded him that he needed to be responsible for his actions. But I noticed that he continued to strive, continued to get his work done, inconsistent as it was. And I noticed something else—a tiredness that wasn't just physical, an emotional fatigue, if you will. It was almost as if he were fighting against a real assailant who was wearing him down bit by bit.

However it wasn't a physical opponent Jeff battled, but his own fears, as he finally revealed to me. He stopped me in the hall one afternoon and said, "I want to tell you I went to see a counselor yesterday. I think it was a good decision to see her, and I couldn't have gone without your help."

I was unclear about how I had contributed to his decision.

"You really helped me when you talked in our class about fear. You mentioned that book *Feel the Fear and Do It Anyway,* and I read it. I realized that I have to face my fears. I can live my life or I can live in fear. Some days when I've missed class, I'll be lying in bed thinking of all the things I'm afraid of and I remember what you said, 'Feel the fear and do it anyway.' That helps me to get up and come to class."

I reminded Jeff that coming to class, facing his fears as he's done, and finally deciding to see a counselor took a lot of courage. I challenged him to look at all the courageous things he'd done instead of focusing on the times his fear had defeated him. He beamed and said very simply, "Thanks."

Again, I'm the one who should have said "Thank you," for Jeff taught me another important lesson. This breakthrough that Jeff had experienced exemplified great tenacity. I've watched other students give up when the pressure became too much, when they got so far behind they couldn't catch up. But Jeff's tenacity, which often manifested itself in too many questions and seemed to irritate other instructors, kept him going. In his questioning he was seeking the clarity he so desperately needed, and he just wouldn't give up until he understood or until he "got it right." Although Jeff continued to be unclear about who he is or what he can do, I believe that it is his persistence in trying to break through his emotional fog and his determination to face his fears that will give him the wings to fly above these dark clouds of doubt.

If anyone needed a way out of darkness, it was Spencer, a thirty-five-year-old man who could barely read or write a complete sentence. Many would label him illiterate, but he was definitely street smart. His tough demeanor, long ponytail, earrings, and leather jacket gave the initial impression of someone I wouldn't want to meet in a dark alley. Even without asking I knew he'd led a wild life prior to coming to college. He'd been in a motorcycle gang, become involved heavily in the drug culture, and had lost most of his money. His turbulent times had taken their toll, for he now experienced severe bouts of depression, often cried during class for no apparent reason, was dangerously overweight, and suffered from narcolepsy.

It didn't take me long to realize that his toughness was a facade, for Spencer was really a very gentle, kind man. Perhaps because he'd made so many mistakes in life, he charged himself to take the younger students under his wing and encourage them to study and apply themselves. I found his efforts particularly poignant because Spencer was severely learning-disabled. He struggled with every new concept and found the simplest learning tasks formidable.

But he was learning to read and was discovering how to write complete thoughts. His excitement was like that of a small child enthralled by ocean waves lapping over his feet.

I once asked him how he'd gotten this far in life with such limited skills. He said, "I faked it."

"How did you ever graduate from high school?" I wondered.

He replied, "The school bribed me. They said if I'd behave, they'd graduate me."

I was appalled and asked him if he were in the least bit angry because no one had ever discovered or addressed his disability. Yes, he was angry, but like so many of my students, he persevered.

He persisted in the face of embarrassment over not being able to read. He kept going even though his wife had to support the family, and his two children were excellent students. And he avoided any situation in which he might be asked to write something as simple as a response to a survey question. Instead he made what little money he could selling hand-made crafts and attended classes faithfully no matter how difficult the course material.

I asked him if he ever got discouraged, if he ever wanted to give up. And his answer was so simple. "Why? Things will work out. They always have."

I was suddenly reminded of the old song about the tiny ant who could move the big rubber tree plant because it had "high hopes." Spencer had hope. The last time I saw him he was ecstatic about his latest endeavor—tutoring other adults who could not read and teaching them about hope.

Whenever I've felt discouraged, I've found myself thinking of two very special students, Monique and David. Monique had a badly deformed body but a beautiful spirit. Her hearing loss and unclear speech made communication very difficult. Yet she never failed to communicate her appreciation of the beauty around her. She loved flowers, drew pictures of gardens, sketched floral designs on her papers, and went into ecstasy when she talked about her visit to Monet's gardens in France. Monique loved nature's splendor and found the plainest tree a thing of beauty. One day she brought me some scarlet and bronze leaves "just because." She may not have learned anything in my class that day, but I did. Monique taught me that beauty is everywhere if you will but look.

Thank goodness for David, the good humor man. He always seemed to be outside my classroom on the very days I needed a good laugh. His sense of humor was subtle, yet powerful. His smile was contagious. He wrote short stories, mysteries mostly, and brought them by for me to read. I could hardly get past the first sentence without laughing out loud. I really looked forward to talking to David, who dismisses his learning disability as "one of those things." He might say that what gets him by is not his philosophy of life, but his philosophy of laugh. It certainly helps me.

I've often wondered why these students I've described fare so well in the face of their special challenges. Why were they able to rise above their difficulties and not be grounded by life's storms? I knew they all worked harder than the average student, learned to compensate for their lack, and practiced the art of filtering out the unimportant. But I felt it was something more that made them exceptional. After observing them for a long time, I concluded that they've done what the old Chinese proverb suggests: "If you can't change your fate, change your attitude."

They simply chose an attitude and went ahead with their lives. Their attitudes—persistence, optimism, excitement, tenacity, humor, appreciation, and hope—helped them soar and find a new perspective. They found freedom in looking down from above. Their problems diminished the higher they rose, so that their predicaments became not weights, but wings.

When I feel weighted down by my own disability—the grind of day-to-day living—I think of Mack or David or Spencer or Shannon and the things they taught me—and my own chair sprouts wings and takes flight.

"The Future Isn't What It Used to Be!"
Benjamin McKeever, Sinclair Community College

If I had my professional life to live over again, I would repent. I would profess nothing, and I would recant everything.

I would not teach the grammatical rules or the rhetorical modes, not even as conventions, because my students never attended those conventions.

I would not teach my students to write with a thesis or a purpose or a motive because very soon they would think that they also needed an alibi and two witnesses.

I would not teach writing as process or writing as product, for writing, like thinking and feeling, believing and knowing, writing, like loving, is a mode of being.

I would know less about errors and expectations, models and maxims, paradigms and promises; and I would know more about teaching and learning.

I would know less about deconstruction and transformation, semiotics and andragogy, and more about the metamorphosis of my students' psyches and the revelation of my students' souls.

I would know less about particles, waves, and fields, pentads and topoi, and more about that which gives my students roots and that which gives my students wings.

I would care less about the facts and more about the truth of my students' lives. I would care less about the mechanics and more about the miracles of my students' essays.

I would care less about the diction and the syntax and more about the credibility and the authenticity of my students' writing; I would care less about their point of view and more about their frame of mind; I would care less about the medium and more about the message of my students' self-understanding.

I would use fewer texts and more contexts; I would ask more questions and offer fewer answers; I would respect silence, welcome dissonance, and encourage tolerance. I would care less about demographic diversity and more about multicultural community.

If I had my composition classes to teach over again, I would shorten my syllabus and lengthen my office hours. I would develop a telephone technique instead of an absence policy. I would provoke more student engagement and accept less student withdrawal.

I would use get-acquainted interviews rather than diagnostic tests. I would use learning contracts instead of grading scales; I would use portfolios in place of pop quizzes. I would use more jokes and anecdotes and fewer myths and shibboleths.

I would be less interested in the left brains or the right brains and more interested in the minds of my students. I would not teach the writing process in terms of planning, drafting, revising, and editing, but in terms compatible with the experience and self-awareness of my students.

I would not mandate free writing, only free thinking. I would not demand attention-getters and clinchers or main ideas and sub-points, only the etiquette of clarity and the decorum of order.

I would not mandate transitions or parallelism, active voice or indicative mood; I would demand only that students write the kind of papers that they would like to read. Titles would be a matter of courtesy, and punctuation an expression of politeness.

I would not police contractions, colloquialisms, or clichés, not even consistency of person, tense, and number. I would counsel awkward constructions and wayward usages, and reform doublespeak and gobbledygook.

I would grant parole to fragments and comma splices, place dangling and misplaced modifiers on probation, and pardon all subject and verb as well as pronoun and antecedent disagreements. I would grant all poems and stories immunity from prosecution.

I would use fewer correction symbols and proofreader's marks—less censure and more praise. I would make more sanguine assumptions about my students' attitude, motivation, and potential; and I would hemorrhage less on my students' essays.

I would imprison only fear and anxiety, writer's block and self-defeat. I would acknowledge each and every small success, nothing more and nothing less.

I would use formative and summative student conferences, holistic group discussions, open-ended questions and students' answers. I would worry less about plagiarism and more about my students' reluctance to speak for themselves.

I would teach writing as an act of caring and sharing. I would not curse the confusion, deplore the chaos, or even notice the noise of my students' meaning-making. I would encourage creative as well as critical thinking and doing one's own thing.

I would not teach the essay as a prince with an introduction, body, and conclusion, and the paragraph as a pauper requiring unity, coherence, emphasis, and completeness. I would teach them as an encounter designed to achieve a meeting of two minds.

I would not argue that writers write best out of their knowledge and experience. I would ask my students to write about something that they wanted to learn about, not about something that they already knew, and tell why and what difference the new knowledge would make to them.

I would ask my students to write about something that they wanted to experience, not about something that they had already experienced, and tell why and what difference the new experience would make to them.

I would not ask my students to write about the great ideas, the cardinal virtues, or even the beatitudes unless they could apply them to the hard scrabble of their daily lives. I would teach the elements of style as if they were the emperor's new clothes—which is really what they ought to be.

I would be less concerned with superteaching and more concerned with superlearning. I would individualize my instruction and compel my students to exercise their freedom to learn in their own way.

I would use a computer network (the alternative is calligraphy), but I would avoid the information superhighway as if it were the primrose path. I would make writing neither digital nor analog, but personal and communal. I would use the computer-mediated classroom, but I would avoid the virtual reality of hyperspace.

I would personalize my instruction and do more troublemaking than troubleshooting. I would accommodate different student learning styles and allow my students to do things their way as well as my way. I would use multimedia, that is, whatever media necessary to reach and teach my students.

I would respond more effectively to my students who could rap but who could not scribe. I would learn to relate to rap, to understand the language of defiance and despair, to learn the pedagogy of the oppressed in the rhymes and runes of this new American poetics.

I would see rap as the act of coming to terms and taking a stand, as that which I have always implored my students to do. I would see rap as the poetry of passion, even lust, for justice. I would see rap as a new take on politics and the English language.

I would encourage my students as writers to "practice random kindness and senseless acts of beauty" to counter the violence of literacy and gangster rap. I would insist that my students say what they mean and mean what they say, but not be mean. I would be on the outlook for insights and congratulate those who would use race as a metaphor rather than a fortress.

I would require my students to know themselves, accept themselves, and be themselves—and then to learn how to learn, to learn how to change, and to learn how to relate.

I would treasure my experience teaching writing to the residents of the human rehabilitation center, where we had the best discussions of social change and criminal justice, and the most enjoyable exercises in sentence-combining and text reconstruction, where writing documented grievances and requests for weekend furloughs as well as letters home to family and friends, and where writing was held in high esteem.

I would pilot more courses and fewer textbooks, believe more in my students and less in my colleagues, and increase my workload instead of my shelf space. I would advocate that we graduate more students with degrees and that we mandate fewer FTE's.

If I had my career in higher education to pursue over again, I would cut to the chase and curtail all preoccupations that did not directly benefit my students.

I would not play the committee game, not even for tenure and promotion. I would not be a professor—assistant, associate, full, or empty. My tenure would be less certain, but more satisfying.

I would attend fewer professional conferences whose themes are always and inevitably the same: "What we know about what we do and what we do about what we know"—and whose conclusions are predictable: That we don't do what we should about what we know because we value our experience too much.

I would conduct fewer workshops on microthemes and microteaching, classroom research and collaborative learning. I would coordinate fewer projects, including Writing Across the Curriculum, which opponents regarded as a conspiracy to augment the corps of English teachers or at least to shirk their work. I would disguise WAC as a movement like civil rights in which everyone of good conscience could become involved.

I would be more active as a faculty mentor and less active as a faculty senator. I would recruit more younger faculty, expand the ranks of parttimers with idealists and pragmatists and maybe a few Baptists—and work to increase their salary.

I would challenge merit pay systems whose criteria were arbitrary and capricious, and faculty performance appraisals whose only standard was proficiency.

I would actually trust the Board of Trustees and regard the Board of Regents as at least nominally competent. I would reread the Mission Statement and check for vital signs of its being accomplished in the college. I would look for the student body, campus culture, and total quality management. I would also look for Utopia, Shangri-La, and El Dorado.

I would remember my own mission to empower my students with the skill and the will to explore their undiscovered selves, and the language to speak their existential truths. I would solicit explanations of Afro soul,

Jewish heart, and Chicano *machismo* as well as receive their take on beauty, truth, and freedom.

I would suspend my belief in cultural literacy until I had determined whose culture and whose literacy. I would concentrate on human values and the value of being human.

I would admit that learning is a mystery, but that students do learn in spite of as well as because of their instructors, and that students learn in more ways than their instructors have to teach them.

I would confess that reading and writing are sources of pain as well as pleasure, but that readers and writers belong to a special community and are engaged in a unique conversation, which my students find enjoyable and rewarding once they learn how to participate.

I would argue that motivation to my students is merely a fancy word for grit and gumption, for "what is it" when "it ain't nothin' but somethin' to do," and that motivation means getting oneself together, doing what one has to do, and taking care of business. I would argue that motivation to them means "the tassel is worth the hassle."

I would observe that education for my students is about ambition and determination, and what they want to be when they grow up, now that they are grown up. I would recognize that to them education means getting credit for what they know, learning what they don't know, and recognizing the difference.

I would acknowledge the wit and wisdom of my students, who have paid their dues as well as their tuition by the time they return to college. They are students who have discovered that "life gives you the test first and then teaches you the lesson afterward." They are students who understandably do not care how much I know until they know how much I care.

If I had my life in the academy to live over again, I would repent to be saved from my own edicts and axioms, conceits and fallacies. I would rediscover teaching and reinvent the teacher; I would remodel learning and redefine the learner. I would admit to having come full circle, but I would argue that life is a school and we are all lifelong learners.

My Most Unforgettable Student

Mary T. Wendrick, Imperial Valley College

Wednesday, 9:10 a.m., sometime in April, my brain is muddled and I'm out of sorts. The end of the semester is coming too fast—again. I've just left my reading class, where everyone was dopey with spring fever, including myself. Office time! A cup of coffee, a chance to put my soul in order and chase away the demons that say "You didn't do enough." Writing class in fifty minutes . . . For now, peace and quiet.

A knock on the door.

"Aaaayyy, Mrs. Weeennnndriiick, how ya dooin?" His brown eyes shine toward a corner just slightly left on my shoulder. Is he here to laugh or to cry?

Tony shuffles his feet; he does that a lot since his brain injury, partly for balance, I guess, and partly because of nervousness.

He acts a little unsure of himself today. Maybe he didn't understand the homework; maybe he's lost his course outline—again; maybe the man in the next row had made fun of him—again; maybe . . . But, no, that's definitely a mischievous look on his face.

He puts his backpack on my chair and pulls out a pink glass rose. "This is for you. I want to thank you for puttin' up with me all the time and helpin' me. I got it in the bookstore. Do you like it? Do you think your husband will get me? Because I'm givin' you a flower?"

"Tony, I love it!"

"I saw it in the bookstore and I asked the lady there if you would like it. She told me the red ones are for girlfriends and so the pink one would be perfect for my teacher. Then, when I got to the cash register, I thought . . . 'My girlfriend! Suuure, I should get a red one for her!' So I did. Wanna see it? Do you think she'll like it?"

He takes my hand. "See ya in class. I wanted to give it to you there, but then everybody would think I was just kissin' up to get a good grade." He kisses my hand and leaves.

The tear I shed drowns my demons. My whole teaching career has been affirmed in that capsule of time by one young man in whose life I know I have made a difference.

Last fall, my husband Mel told me Tony was tired of marking time here at the college. He had been taking therapeutic physical education and getting re-socialized for the past year. He had been retraining his brain, trying to re-store the ideas and facts he had lost in a motorcycle accident. But he was bored; he wanted more. Mel directs the program for disabled students and he wondered if Tony could try a mainstream writing class at a very basic level. We decided to talk with him about it, so his counselor sent him to me to see if he was ready to cope with a regular Monday, Wednesday, Friday writing class in basic composition, mostly paragraphs and grammar. Tony was will-ing, eager, and bursting with hope.

I was afraid. What if he failed? How would that affect him? My hus-band had told me that this young man had moments and days of severe de-pression, days when he wanted to kill himself, days when he could recall somehow that he was no longer the Tony he had been before his accident. Somedays he could remember that he used to be quick, athletic, bright, devil-may-care. Then, he would look at his damaged gait, his slow, slow, slow achievements, his frustrations. Tears would stream down his face, and he would cry out that he couldn't make it.

But if he couldn't even have the chance . . . how would that affect him? So, we all agreed—Tony, his counselor, my husband, and I—that Tony would take a placement test like everyone else to see if he was eligible for the class. We explained that he might have to take the test more than once. He listened very seriously; then he wrote a short essay about someone he ad-mired. It was sent over to me for my judgment. I didn't want to read it. But Tony was watching me every time I walked across campus; he was waiting for my decision. I had to read it. And be honest.

It wasn't perfect; it needed work, but it was simple and coherent. Tony admired Richie, a young tutor who would listen to people and give them the help they requested. Tony obviously had retained or regained some language skills. But the question remained: Could he handle the stress of regular class meetings, with classroom routines, with other students, with deadlines . . . ?

Once again a summit meeting, with Tony there, too. Try it, get help, have a notetaker, ask for help when you need it. See what happens. Remember, many students coming back to school for the first time need to repeat classes until they get adjusted to the routine. "Yes, Maam, okay, Maaaaam, I'll do it."

Tony sits in the front seat, next to the wall, with his notetaker right be-hind him. He does all the work, he asks questions sl-oo-oo-ww-lly. His hand-writing takes forever but is more legible than mine. Tony's notetaker, Juan, could handle the final drafts, but Tony thinks Juan's writing style is not good enough. He wants the finished product to look good, even if it takes him several days to finish it. He loves to joke and to answer questions.

But his moods are unpredictable.

Sometimes he comes to my office and cries because he can't remember things. He learns the homework and forgets it. It's hard to convince him that he's experiencing the normal learning process, or that he's forgetting more than the other students have yet learned! It's hard to remind him that all of us forget and that some of the rules don't matter because he still can express himself verbally better than many others. He wants to be better than himself!

He writes another essay about a man he admires. He tells me my husband always takes time to listen to his problems. One day, he even went swimming with Tony to help him overcome his fear of the water. I show the assignment to Mel, who tells me the rest of the story. Tony used to be able to swim very well. After the accident, he couldn't coordinate the stroke and the breathing. When Mel went with him to the pool, he encouraged Tony to try to swim the width; he made it halfway, stood up and began to cry. Mel and the swimming instructor provided Tony with a snorkel and fins and had him try again. Now he swims the length of the pool in twenty-seven seconds.

One day, a young man stays after class to explain why he's been absent and not concentrating on his work. Tony's hanging around like he does sometimes. Rafael tells me his sister-in-law has been in a terrible accident. She was thrown out of her vehicle and has suffered a head injury. She's been in a coma for two weeks and is now just coming out of it. He's been helping with the children.

Tony listens carefully; this is his territory now; he's the expert in this field. Soon the two young men are comparing notes. Tony is giving encouragement to Rafael, whose sister-in-law is so much better already than Tony is after years. For the first time, I hear Tony's story. "I was drunk—and stoned—and I wasn't wearing my helmet, either. I had it, but I wasn't wearing it. I was speeding, too, when I hit that tree in Mexicali. When I woke up—months later, I saw this white light all around me. It was the hospital walls. I thought I was in heaven, but I knew that wasn't right, because I was supposed to be in hell!" He looks at me to see if I've noticed his joke.

I smile, but inside I'm acknowledging that Tony is in hell—a lot. I've seen and heard him there. He hasn't yet reprogrammed the defenses that hide his ups and downs from others. He's not ashamed to talk to his counselor, to Mel, or to me, and he's not too proud to listen. In a way, I hope he never does relearn those skills. My rapport with Tony came about easily because of his trust in Mel and in his other counselors, but I know that he counts on me to affirm that he can succeed. I will always remember that while I affirm his potential, he is affirming mine.

The Climb

Vincent G. Barnes, Shoreline Community College

The end of a purple and green rope. A hundred feet of vertical sandstone below. The aluminum 'biners on my belt clink like tin chimes, the sound soon lost in the expanse of the windblown pinnacle. Pinched in a pink and blue stub of a shoe, one foot quivers violently, refuses to respond, yet finally twists onto a sixteenth-inch lip of shoddy stone. The other dangles, useless given the scarcity of footholds. One hand paws at a mere depression; the other locks desperately on a chicken head, as climbing jargon refers to protrusions. "Sparrow head" seems a more accurate description.

A new perception reigns. In the same way that anything organic becomes nourishment to a starving person, I now see even pea-sized pebbles, cemented in place with the glue of the ages, as the steps to deliverance, if my strength holds until I reach Mike at the top. A wiry, silent man about my age, Mike was my student in English 100. Now it is his turn to teach me a lesson.

The seeds for this predicament were sown as I planned my syllabus half a year earlier. For lack of a better idea, I had organized the reading and writing course around rhetorical forms, with a selection of essays including description, comparison/contrast and process analysis. For his process essay, Mike choose to write about some aspect of rock climbing; it might have been "How to rig a belay." On the appointed day, I collected the papers and carried them home in my worn satchel for the ritual so many evenings seem devoted to: grading papers. Mike's came up somewhere in the middle. I could tell he had tried, since climbing was something he was passionate about, but the paper fell well short. I pictured him up late at night finishing it, tangled in a knot of unfamiliar words, trying to summon something presentable out of the pile of concepts, instructions, and models I had dumped on him and his classmates. I imagined scratch marks in the dust on his desk as he exhausted the last of his energy and let his hands slip to his sides in resignation.

To divert attention from the paper's inadequacies, I wrote on the last page that while the paper lacked certain essential components, it had at least piqued my curiosity about rock climbing. I added in slightly smaller print that I would like to try climbing myself. I could not really think of anything else to say. The next day, I gave the papers back in the hasty, even brusque manner that possesses me when grades are low. Mike approached me after class. He seemed unfazed by the low grade, but quite pleased that I was interested in climbing. He said he would be glad to show me some basic rock climbing. We would go one day in the summer, he promised.

Throughout the quarter, none of Mike's papers showed much sign of improvement. I told myself that there was always the possibility that what Mike didn't seem to have grasped in class could emerge spontaneously at a later date, but I didn't really believe it. He looked to me for help in his silent way, and I did what I could under the constraints of time and fatigue, but my commitment was tempered by the unspeakable notion that perhaps Mike was just not meant to be in college. He passed marginally, then dropped out of school. Apparently mine was not the only class he struggled through.

I could have empathized more with Mike. For me it had been geometry. I remember the day I quit. It was the *first* day of class. I felt that dread, that sinking, sickening frustration that comes when one shares neither the language nor even the basic assumptions of everyone else, like a visitor to another, very different culture. My lack of understanding began with the instructor's first sentence. It was downhill from there. With the tools of my Humanities training, I rationalized: Math was evil, anyway. It was a tool of the corrupt techno-industrial complex that would lead to the destruction of the world as we know it, a bundle of arrows in the quiver of some Apollonian constellation presiding over an epoch of war and excess.

Unlike Mike, however, I did not drop out, for while I might have failed at math, I was moderately agile in at least one medium that academia recognizes and endorses: reading and writing. With these skills to fill my sails through college, I was able to navigate well clear of math's angular reefs, which might have ripped open my fragile ego to expose the incomplete ribbing of my knowledge. By the time I finished college, I'd forgotten my failure at math—or repressed it—and emerged basking opulently in the security of a degree officially sanctioned by the academic community as representing real knowledge: a degree in prose writing, with a mandate to elevate and edify the masses who, less fortunate—less well endowed, perhaps—got the notion to try higher education. There would of course be losers: those not meant to win, like Mike.

At Pinnacle Peaks rock climbers' park, sandstone sentinels mark the boundary between the unredeemable sagebrush hills of arid Eastern Washington and the lush, productive orchard country along the margins of the Wenatchee River, fattened on Cascade snowfall, winding out of the mountains to rendezvous with the Columbia. With fruited branches drooping lazily in the late summer heat, the orchards flaunt an arrogant fecundity at the parched, wanting sagebrush above, the trees' vigor attributable, of course, to innate superiority, rather than providential location on a river bank. On weekends, climbers festoon the cliffs of the pinnacles with their vibrant ropes, testing their mettle on the boundary between the sagebrush and the orchards.

We park in the parking lot, sling our gear on our backs and hike up the switchbacks that connect the pinnacles. We stop below an expanse of stone, once horizontal layers of lake bed, now thrust into the vertical by the ineluctable forces of an unwitnessed geologic revolution. This slab is named Martian Tower.

"Let's try this," Mike says in his succinct English. Rock climbing requires nothing more, nor less. Of course I have objections, which I do not voice. I am a beginner at this; I need to enter it slowly, experience successes, build confidence. But now I can not say anything, probably for the same reasons Mike had never protested the assignments I gave. He just did them and waited for the consequences. I am sorry I let on that I fancied myself an athlete with a natural-born affinity for things outdoor.

At the foot of this massif, Mike is no longer the tentative, worried scholar entering a process of doubt. The man who had slipped, slid, even tumbled down the slopes of the most modest of academic inclines takes charge. He scans the expanse, analyzing the sheet of empty rock. He visualizes a route, conceptualizes a geometry of body angles, estimates type and number of cams and slings he will need to reach the belaying point at the top. In his silent assessment, he demonstrates confidence and competence in a half dozen practical applications of theories that had sunk him in college. He slips into his harness, and in a flourish ties in. He breathes deeply, dips his hands into his chalk bag, rubs them together, claps once and waits for the puff of chalk dust to evaporate, then places his palms against the stone, firmly and respectfully, like a surgeon pressing on a patient's back.

"Climbing," he tells me.

"Climb on," I reply hesitantly, unfamiliar with this new jargon. He starts and ascends in a rhythm of seamless moves, coaxing hand and toe holds out of bare rock, his body a remarkable integration of applied engineering principles: stress, compression, friction, and tension: geometry in motion. Quickly reaching the top, he rigs a belay by calculating the angle of greatest stress in the event of a fall and hastily distributes the pull across several pieces of protection that he wedges into unlikely cracks in the rock.

Now it is my turn. I imitate Mike's ritual with the chalk, but inhale the dust cloud. Coughing, I pat the rock and begin. The pitch is easy at first, as simple as constructing a short paragraph, in language any kid weaned on monkey bars could manage. Soon, though, there is nothing left to hold on to. I can not go down because then Mike would have no way to get down without abandoning expensive equipment at the top. I begin to panic. Mike starts his directions. He tells me how I can smear my shoe here, counter-thrust there. The little sixteenth-inch lip will, he says, hold me. With his encouragement, and attentive tension on the rope, I take my very modest strength, transfer it down-tendon and lock my fingers into small cracks or onto pebbles and in combination with my toes, move my whole body excruciatingly upward. Ungracefully, I squirm. My legs road-runner.

Of course I fall, but I'm always stopped quick when Mike jams the rope tight in his belaying tool. My life depends on him in a direct way, this rope an umbilicus. I reach Mike finally, my dignity and pride bruised like fallen fruit, but I manage at least to leave the debacle with a lesson.

From geometry, I should never have forgotten that we are all developmental students, but the successful among us manage to hide it. From the security of expertise in accepted fields, we deliberately avoid contexts where our knowledge is useless, thus avoiding any articulation of our uselessness. We create a fictive self unsusceptible to the frailty of ignorance or incompetence. Those without recognized academic skills enjoy no such luxury. For them, college is one affirmation after another of their inadequacy. They have no place to hide in college.

Dangling from the rope, I had no place to hide, no way to camouflage my weakness. Yet there was a difference, for the rope was tangible. I could trust it not to break. More importantly, I could trust Mike at the top to apply tension or slack the rope when I needed it, to provide direction, to watch, and to literally catch me when I fell. I could climb the rock face, but it was not because the skill was innate; I needed the rope and Mike guiding me. With shame, I realized the rope I held for Mike in his venture into the steep, unfamiliar terrain of academia was not as fast as the one he held for me on the rock when I slipped. How could I have expected him to succeed in the face of my suspicious and incomplete support?

The lesson crystallizes as resolution: I must not forget my own fallibility beyond the walls of academia, and for all of us humility seems worthy of salvage from the era's junkyard of abandoned values. I must also remember that Mike's practical knowledge in its own context was no less valid than the theoretical formulae we worship in college. I'll encourage Mike to get more of his professors out on the rock; it would do them good. Most importantly, in my English classes as I talk my students up the precipices of rhetoric, I will not forget the power that held me in my own ascent; lives depend on the rope I extend in the classroom, as well.

Breathing the Words:
What Students Have Taught Me
Susan Streeter Carpenter, Antioch College

From just reading students' papers, I've learned things I wouldn't otherwise know: about skeet-shooting, graffiti art, basketball heroes, the cultural impact of Nirvana's first video. A student showed me the almost-ecstasy, almost-death of shooting up on heroin. I've witnessed, through a painfully large number of students, the nail-hard process of recovery from alcohol addiction and the black holes in the lives of people who've been sexually abused. I've learned what it's like to be a dancer-choreographer, to be a Japanese child, to be Muslim, to be gay. I still fix mashed potatoes the way a student taught me.

This is the Course for People Who Hate Writing, though it has different names: Developmental English, Expository Writing, Writing Skills Workshop, English 101. Hatred of writing, I've learned from my students, is not simple. The act itself, stringing words together, one after another, is fraught with demons. Old teacherly voices, parental expectations, your own most foolish, stupid, and angry thoughts rise up out of the dark when you sit down at the desk. Add resentment for having been placed in the "remedial" class; add distrust of the words themselves; add the distractions of what students often call "the stresses of modern fast-paced life." It's impressive that they manage to write anything, yet virtually all of them do.

Write what you care about, I tell every class; *you're going to revise so many times you'll get bored silly if you're not writing about something that matters to you.*

Some of them don't believe me at first; they hold out hope that I won't require a revision this time (*But it's in the syllabus*, I say: *minimum three complete revisions of each paper*), or they write cautious, boring essays. Sam, a high school coach, wrote three pages which mostly informed the reader that baseball, football, and basketball are all indeed played with balls. William wrote for eight weeks about golf.

When the words are blocked by demons, fogged by distractions, choked by frustration, freewriting helps. *No one sees this page but you*, I tell the class; *you are free to burn it the minute you're done. You are free to write any words that pop into your mind. **Any** words.* The process works for most students—and I use freewriting, myself, to understand what's going on:

*Right now I notice sounds: the hum of the heater, the distant voice of the professor down the hall, the nearby voices of pencils and hands moving across paper. I want to write with this class; it feels safer than usual—because the group is small? It feels as though all our pencils are connected. Maybe this is my feeling, **my** need to be connected with people.*

I know that when people write together they help each other by the writing itself, as well as by the reading and the listening. I want help with my writing, these days. I want quiet, pen-scratchy ten-minute blocks to write in. I want the sense of time slowing down. I want the comfort of stringing words together one at a time.

Right now I notice that I'm probably too comfortable to be writing very well. The good stuff comes when I am on the edge of tears, breathing the words—and what do I mean by that?

So this is the course where we learn to scribble again. But this is also the course where we deal with grammar, where we use constructs—participial phrase, non-restrictive clause, parallel structure—that exist only here in the land of written Standard English, not in the wide world. Complete sentences may be necessary to get through college, the students concede. "I'll never use it, of course, once I've got the degree," a man said recently. Maybe he's right; he's got such an important job he carries his beeper and his cellular phone to class.

At first I "taught" grammar and punctuation, and as a result I learned the terms and constructs pretty well. I watched students pass tests easily while the sentences in their essays remained garbled. I read clear, more-or-less correct essays from students who could not pass the grammar tests. It was a relief to stop testing. For awhile I stopped dealing with grammar in class at all. I'm still going back and forth about this issue.

"You see," students say, "I write like I talk." This means, I've learned, *I think like I talk. I can't think like I don't talk.* Even people who've spoken English their whole lives, even people who've grown up in the suburbs, distrust Standard English. They can't imagine fitting their own honest musings, reflections, opinions, analyses—much less their experiences—into the kind of language which distinguishes between "who" and "whom," the language of textbooks and newscasters. And who else? Who, in this culture of selling and consuming, packaging and hype, uses language to say straightforwardly what they mean?

A multitude of writers do, of course; once you start looking, there they are. But I rely on students to show me how grammar matters. An eighteen-year-old artist from central Philadelphia explained, "I like to use language creatively, so the rules don't apply."

"I've seen your sketches," I said. "You have terrific control over your pen. Don't you want the same kind of control over your writing? Knowing sentence structure and punctuation gives that to you." Two days later he was in my office pumping me for grammar, punctuation, and word use, rapid-firing questions and sucking up answers until I was dizzy, wondering if I'd chosen the right worksheets, the best pages in the book.

Mechanics, after all, are connected to—bound up in—meaning. Rosemary had returned to school after twenty-some years of keeping the books for her husband's business. Her essays—about a close friend who'd died from cancer, about a Las Vegas vacation, about her daughter and granddaughter—were fine, after she'd revised them several times, but the tenses kept changing in odd, arbitrary ways.

"You need to clear up these tense shifts," I told her. "Just go through and check all the verbs." I showed her the pages in the book, and she could see, yes, past, present, and future, with their variations; it all made sense. But somehow studying her own pages was not the same. How could she be so confused among her own words?

It's hard to see clearly what you've written, I've learned from students (and from readers' noting flaws in my own writing). Thoughts travel mysterious routes from their vague, three-dimensional, half-formed state across the left brain and out to form words, one after another. Even after you've translated and reconstructed them into sentences, correctly punctuated, parts of the original experience cling to the words on the page in a way that you can't escape, and an objective reader can't see.

For Rosemary, the clinging experience—and the way it had confused her tenses—was particularly graphic. The last day of class came. To pass the course, she had to write a final essay on the spot—and she still had to straighten out the tenses in the other three. Cornered, red in the face, she sat down, wrote the title, "Betrayal," and went to work. Two hours later she handed in a pain-filled story which began with the discovery that her husband had been having an affair with her closest friend. Ever since, the essay explained, she'd been reconstructing her understanding of the world from scratch. Writing about her late friend, describing Las Vegas, discussing her daughter's life may have been part of the process. *Naming* what had happened, telling it straight out, seemed to give her the power to see clearly again past, present, and future. While I read "Betrayal," she went through her other three essays and corrected the tenses. Perfectly. We were finished at the same time.

The restraints of grammar and punctuation sometimes knot and snarl the strings of words. When you've made sentences into tight boxes with no room to stretch, freewriting helps.

Katrin, a German exchange student, holds up her little stubby pencil. "Do you have something that will put away the wood?" She scrapes at the stubbiness with her fingers.

"Pencil sharpener," I say. "In my office."

"Thanks," she says, and goes.

Pencil sharpener. Solid. hard to find solidity these days, especially in writing. I look at my story, which I've been scraping away at so carefully for so long, putting away the wood in little shavings, trying to get down to the "quick," the place where it lives, clean and clear as a flame. And the lines on the page waver: is this sentence quick or dead—or dying? Can it be revived? If I scrape off this word—"so"—will I kill it?

And now all sentences, all strings of words, even this one, even the aimless lines on this page, have a particular kind of trembling, wavering life under my pen. I write "trembling, wavering" like that, and feel the thump of an artery close to the skin.

Somehow, in every class, students get through the fear and loathing to the power which writing can unleash. The argument essays arrive about midterm, and the very word "argument," even after I've explained the academic meaning, invokes vehemence. A couple of years ago, for example, there was a spate of papers blaming Columbus for all the oppression and injustice since 1493, including modern environmental problems and AIDS—or that's what they seemed to be doing; it was hard to tell. They were confusing as ever, full of the same old mistakes. When I read such stuff halfway through the course, I wonder if I've told students the truth about their having something important to say, if I've had any impact on their motivation to write clearly—to think clearly.

After William finished his third golf essay, he handed in something called "The Selling of America," which bashed not only the Japanese but foreigners of all but blue-blood Yankee stock, tore into women who supported the right to abortion, and managed to accuse several other groups of conspiring to rob self-respecting Americans (whoever he thought we were) of all their mountain majesties and fruited plains. I wrote careful notes in the margins—*How do you know this? Explain further. What does this have to do with your subject?*—and passed it back. His revision was worse. *He must be angry at me*, I thought.

When you no longer know how to say anything useful to your students, education specialists say, open up. Take a deep breath and risk being vulnerable. And freewriting helps. Clean out of ideas for the Columbus-bashing class, I decided (inhale) I'd read aloud whatever came to me during freewriting time (exhale).

Last week I spent every morning working on an essay I'd promised to write last year. I've probably spent twenty hours on this essay (plus at least forty hours avoiding the essay, frittering time) and I'm still not happy with it. Yesterday I took it to the editor at the local paper & told her how I felt.

"I'm sure I'll like it," she said. "Do you want me to call you and tell you so anyway?"

"Yes," I said. She hasn't called.

This morning an agent said, "I really like your writing." Which was good to hear, but she'd rejected my six novel chapters, and she didn't invite me to send her the book again after I'd finished it.

I didn't expect to tell you about my hard times. I was going to write about the experience of reading your papers, how they sound to me, and what seems to be the seventh-week zeitgeist here.

But I see now what I should say to you: LISTEN. You—all and each one—are good writers. Keep going. I know you didn't want it to be this frustrating. Neither did I. But don't give up.

Because some of your papers (or the voices I think I hear between the lines of them) sound tired and discouraged. You sound like you've had enough of caring about comma splices and correct spelling and clarity clarity clarity.

Listen, words for me are like little keys opening miles and miles of locked doors and letting out secret after secret after secret.

I want to give you the keys.

I wish it were that simple.

"Awesome," the students said afterward, and their next papers were somewhat better, which they probably would have been anyway. I keep learning: student papers do get better. I keep learning: the tighter the corner you're in, the greater the pressure to go through the wall, to risk something which would have seemed crazy otherwise. Breakthroughs are very good for writing.

I called William in for a conference to find out if he was angry. No, he said, he'd just been having a hard time expressing himself. But he'd written something new, which he handed across the desk. It was a description of the coal town in West Virginia where he was born, of wood smoke and a river and small-town streets friendly to a child. Before he was grown, the coal company had decided the mine was not lucrative enough and pulled out. William described in detail the death of the town.

"Is there a relationship," I asked him, "between the coal company and these Japanese businesses you've written about in 'The Selling of America'?" The parallel hadn't occurred to him, but he could see the connection. "Suppose," I said, "a Japanese person bought the farm next to you and proceeded to live there and raise crops. Would you have a problem with that?" No problem with that, William said. "Suppose," I went on, "a guy from California came in, bought the land, developed it into a shopping center and then let it go down. Who are you really angry at, foreigners or absentee landlords?" The final version of "The Selling of America" became a rational diatribe against absentee landlords, almost as effective as the essay about the death of a home town.

Think of writing as a chance to practice taking risks, an act of courage, I tell my students. *Fear is where the power is.* Some of them take this advice and run with it, far down the field.

Sam, as bored with his balls-in-sports paper as I was, stuck his head into the office. "I lost another kid," he said. "She was murdered. I think I better write about her." Later, he told me, the flood of anger and grief had almost engulfed him as he wrote—but it was worth doing. Wasn't it?

Of course. Isn't it always?

This is the course where students read their work aloud to each other. A young man, Joshua, read his essay to the class; it was long, full of double negatives, profanity, and abstractions. "Did you get it?" he asked the other students. And they tried to report what they'd understood.

"It was hard," one said. "I've never used drugs, but I can understand how it would be." The scene where Joshua and Jennifer shoot heroin was the most vivid, they agreed, more or less clear to them all.

If this essay were a painting, I asked, what would it be? "Steel," said one.

"Jackson Pollock," said another.

"Oh no," Joshua said. "Jackson Pollock? Not even Hieronymus Bosch?" And he told them—told us—about being a recovering junkie, how completely heroin takes over, how hard it is to give up. Every single hungry-for-junk cell has to be slowly shed and replaced. "Do you understand the last past of the essay?" he asked insistently. "Is there hope? Do you think there's hope at the end?"

Of course, they all said. There's always hope, isn't there?

In writing about the death of a youngster in a Midwestern city high school, Sam had begun to use writing as more than a necessity for getting through college. He wrote another essay comparing his kids with street children of the same age in Da Nang twenty-five years ago. And then . . . then, on Grand Reading Day, when everyone in class read their last, presumably their best work, Sam read an account of one soldier's experience in Vietnam. The detail was cruel and vivid, and none of us was surprised when he revealed that he himself was that soldier. He'd found it too hard to write in first person, he said; he had never written these experiences before. But by then we were all in tears. Sam too.

Sometimes I wonder if writing is important after all. Just because I love it doesn't mean it's essential—people go for years of their adult lives without writing anything beyond shopping lists and their signatures. I know that. And some things I read—even published works—make me think, *just as well we don't all believe we can write.* And many of my own writings remind me of Jackson Pollock's paint dribbles and splotches.

So I keep signing up to teach the class for people who fear and loathe writing. You'd think I'd get tired of it, and I do—but it's exhaustion, not boredom. Right now, for example, I'm dealing with an essay calling for a repeal of the constitutional amendment which gave women the vote. Another student has given me the chance to vicariously swim with dolphins. A health-conscious student's essay has convinced me to drink more water, and I'm feeling better.

Listen, students give me keys which open miles and miles of locked doors, letting out secret after secret after secret.

The Blue Chair

Sandra M. Jensen, Linn-Benton Community College

I am in despair as I write to you this morning. A fine gray mist sifts over the green Willamette fields. The mustard saturates my eyes with saffron yellow as it undulates away into stands of white oak and Douglas fir. This morning, black-headed grosbeaks made their first appearance in the valley, and yesterday we saw an immature black-shouldered kite flashing white over the racing blue hood of the car. We just caught a glimpse of its eye before it curved sharply up into free space.

My school, Linn-Benton Community College, sprawls spaciously among these early May fields. In the courtyard, a warm spring sun illumines the drenched burnt-crimson of the rhododendrons. My office is on the second floor of the Takena Building. It is two and a half yards by three yards and is shared by five part-time English teachers. I teach one class on Monday, Wednesday, and Friday. To get here, I commute an hour each way on unwaveringly straight I-5 down the valley where the pioneers found their golden promise at the end of the Oregon Trail. My monthly paycheck is $324.00.

In my office are two desks, some file cabinets, a bookcase, two chairs for teachers, and one chair for visiting students. It is this chair, turquoise molded fiberglass on bent metal legs, that is the source of the morning's black mood. I have just said good-bye to Kimi, who came in to tell me she is dropping my class. Kimi is seventeen years old with a GED. She is a skinny kid with springy red hair, splotchy freckles and smart green eyes. Today she was dressed in rags: torn hightop sneakers; snagged leotard; an unwashed, tie-dyed shirt. Jittery, jumpy, twitchy, she looked like Pippi Longstocking on drugs.

"Mrs. Jensen, I just got out of Alcohol and Drug Rehab in March. I dunno. I guess I got too ambitious and thought I could take on the world with all these classes."

"But Kimi, you were doing fine with your writing. Why do you have to drop?"

Teeth chattering, body twitching, Kimi said, "Mrs. Jensen, I guess I'm having a little problem with my sobriety." Why are you telling me this, Kimi? Do I look like your counselor?

Jana was in that same chair last Wednesday. Jana is a mother of three now returning to school after her husband left her. She's hoping to be a dental hygienist, but she explains that she has to drop my Writing 115 class, too. "My sister was murdered in Salem, and they just caught the guy. I have to appear at the trial as a witness." Her brown eyes are full of the held-back tension of determinedly unshed tears, and all I can find to say is, "I understand." But I know I don't; I couldn't possibly understand. I'm not her therapist.

Nina also sat in the blue chair last week. She's a beautiful woman in her forties with four children and a first grandchild. With her long, straight, black hair and Chinese/Irish beauty, she still looks like a likable kid herself, except for the black eyes and the bruises along one side of her face and down her arm. "I had a court order against him, Mrs. Jensen, and the first time he attacked me I called 911, and they put him in jail. But he was released because they needed the cell space. Nobody called to tell me he was out. He came straight to my apartment, broke in, and beat me up. Now he's in a car across the street. Everywhere I go, he follows me. I don't know how, but I have to disappear. I really like your class, Mrs. Jensen, but I'm afraid he's going to kill me."

What am I supposed to say? "But Nina, you were doing so well with your pronoun reference problems."

Blue chair, blue chair, whatever happened to Alicia, who sat there explaining her problem to me after being gone most of the quarter? She had had stomach flu the first day that she didn't come to class. She had been dropping someone off at the local airstrip, and on the way home from the Lebanon Airport, she had pulled over to throw up in a ditch. A man in a pick-up stopped as if to offer to help and then raped her right there in the irrigation ditch among the lovely yellow mustard and Alicia's viral vomit. She threw up right on him, and she still got pregnant. The worst that could have happened to him is that he got the flu.

Alicia didn't drop the class, but she wrote an essay about getting raped. It was full of grammar and punctuation and organizational errors, and because I'm a good teacher, do you think I flunked Alicia? You know, she didn't attend much class the last few weeks of the term after the abortion, and she had a hard time focusing on her verb tenses.

Laurel slept every class in the front row. Finally, she told me it was because she couldn't sleep at night because her boyfriend had been stalking her for weeks. I took her to the library. I literally put her hands on the keys of the database computer. "Type, Laurel. Write 'anti-stalking laws' and push 'enter.'" A nineteen-year-old, blonde zombie on tranquilizers, Laurel pushed through the fog and wrote her research paper on what she could do about being stalked. I saw her pursuer waiting outside the library. I got used to seeing his dusty white Camaro outside the classroom window. Laurel learned what Nina already knew, that she could get a court order. She left the class bright, with a new idea, followed by her lethal shadow. I never saw her on campus again, and she never came by to pick up her "A" paper. I have no idea what happened to her, and Nina's story doesn't encourage me to suppose the best. But she's a successful student, and isn't that what really counts in this profession? And anyway, I'm not her mother.

Julie's a success story, too. Julie and her fiance were both on the Mt. Bachelor Ski Patrol. On a mid-term weekend, they were doing the last sweep of the slopes together. The heavy spring snow cut loose above the tree line and roared down the steep, narrow run Brad was sweeping, and Brad got swept. Julie's classroom journal faithfully recorded the details of his death, how they recovered his body in pieces by digging in the places where the snow was bright red, his funeral, the grief of her almost-in-laws, her own thoughts of suicide. Her research report on a snow safety program for kids was late, but I waived my late-papers policy, and she got an "A." Julie is a successful student who knows how to manage her time.

I wish I knew how to tell you that I'm not exaggerating. I wish I could tell you in your far-off place that not all the stories I hear from the blue chair are from women, although most of them are. To balance the equation, I should mention Keith McCrory. We had been reading about slaves being whipped. Keith said, "You can't imagine what that feels like. All you want to do is die."

"Oh, and what do you know about it?" challenged another male student. Keith, who works in the Salem legislature and is going to school to be a paralegal, stripped off his tie and shirt and showed us the keyloided web of long, lash-mark scars on his back. "My Dad beat me and my brother with willow sticks soaked in salt water."

I should mention sixteen-year old Scott, who also dropped the class last week because, "Oh, Mrs. Jensen, I guess maybe I smoke a little too much dope. I just can't seem to focus this term. Maybe I'll be back in the fall." Or the father who told me he had chained his son to the bed, which was then locked in a closet, because his son was selling dope at Crescent Valley High School (perhaps to a bright sixteen-year-old named Scott, who was starting college early). Tell me, what category does *that* story fit into?

Annie drove out from Kansas with her dog Fathom ("I call him Fathom because he's so deep") to join her boyfriend and go to school at LBCC. The boyfriend was living with another woman, and now Annie is living in her car because no one will rent to her and Fathom. Why are you telling me this, Annie; do I look like your social worker?

Elizabeth's ex-husband bribed their two boys to drive her to a park, lock her in their van, and abandon her. The police found her, and now she's finishing the class from a safe house in Bend. She's completely deaf because her husband said, "I'll beat you about the head and ears if you try to go back to school," and did. Elizabeth learned sign language and gets tutorial help through the Learning Disabilities Program.

When do I stop telling these stories? Why are there so many to tell? People move to rural Oregon from all over the country because the "quality of life" is rated so highly by all the magazines. But a harsh, daily violence soaks this green and gentle land with private grief, private blood, private stories. We are an open-enrollment school, and these are the people who flood through our doors.

There are three weeks left in the term, and I have maybe five or eight students left out of an enrolled twenty-four. It doesn't matter to me, of course. I stare at the empty, blue chair. I'll still get paid $324.00 at the end of the month.

Puttles and the Trauma of the Predicate
Charlotte Langford, Pima Community College

"Sick with Flew. pleas don't drop me." The note was signed "Paula Franz."

"Really sick," I wondered as I walked into class, "or just too nervous?" The first day seems to be the toughest for developmental writing students. They straggle in, carrying enormous backpacks filled with new books (one of which will be the wrong edition of our text), a sandwich, several pens, a pencil that will never sharpen, a candy bar, a sack of corn nuts which some-one in the back row will eat noisily later in the hour while I'm trying to explain the first important point of the course. They are silent and look at no one, especially not at me. After finding a pen and tearing several sheets of paper out of a spiral notebook, they wait, lambs at the slaughter.

I call the roll, struggling with the names: "Mahnaz Sadatmousavi. How do you pronounce your name?"

"Oh, any way, that was fine." The beautiful dark-headed woman looks up briefly and then concentrates again on the desk in front of her.

"Maria Josephina. Where are you?" I see a hand raised briefly. "What name do you like to be called? Or do you have a nickname?"

"Anything. Any name is fine, Ma'am."

I stumble on. It's only after several weeks that I learn the truth: Maria Josephina is always Josie, and you pronounce the *h* in *Mahnaz* like *ha*. I also discover that Raymond prefers the name RJ; the sweet kid on the back row whom I've been calling Mike is, in reality, Michael; Amelia goes by her middle name, Clara; and Tiffany is called Tippy.

It is not that these reticent scholars don't care about their names, or that I am an ogre; developmental students just feel so temporary in the class-room, so out of place, so needy. They do not dare ask for anything except the knowledge they've come for, and then it's a yes/no proposition: yes, I want to learn, but, no, I can't take a test on punctuation today.

After roll call on the first day, I ask my group of wary strangers to tell something about themselves. At this moment, although they don't know it, we begin our journey, twenty-seven souls, together for a semester, making mistakes, making friends, making connections, teaching and learning. And I don't necessarily mean that I'll be doing all the teaching, and they all the learning.

A tall woman in the second row speaks up first. "My name is Francie and I'm coming back after ten years. I dropped out of high school. I've got three kids and I'm a single parent."

"Hey! You dropped out of high school? Me too." A sad-faced girl near the window leans forward and the two share a long, pained smile. Another woman chimes in."You've got three kids? I've got two and one on the way."

"My name is Jerry and myself and my family just moved here from Jersey and I've played in a band."

"Hey man! What instrument? I play drums. What's your favorite group?"

"Guitar. Bon Jovi."

After a long quiet spell, I call out to a woman in the back row. "Hi. Won't you tell us a little about yourself? Andrea, was it?"

"Yes. My name is Andrea."

"Have you got a favorite story about yourself, or a hobby you enjoy?"

"No. Not really." Silence. We move on.

"Hello. I'm Fred. I'm working thirty hours a week, just got married, and am taking writing, math, and psychology. I didn't graduate from high school either."

"My name is José." The older man's dark, friendly eyes peer around the room. "I'm seventy-two years old and looking for a new career. You'll have to speak up because my hearing aid broke and I don't have no money to get a new one. May I have your permission to sit on the front row?"

"I'm Teresa. My husband beat me up and broke both my arms. He's in prison now. I have to learn new job skills because my hands don't work right any more." She holds up her arms and we see the long white scars snaking down toward her wrists. "I have five children."

"Hi! I'm Beverly, and I'm an alcoholic. I go to two meetings a day. What time do we take a break in this class? I'm not giving up cigarettes!"

"My name is Jason. I've been in a wheelchair all my life. I have M.S. and I plan to be an engineer."

"I am Tamad. I am from Yemen. Does anyone here know where is Yemen? I have brought a map."

"William here." The tall restless young man runs freckled fingers through tufts of red hair. "My brains are fried by drugs. If I act weird in class, I don't mean any harm by it, okay?"

"Hello. My name is Tanya. I am from Russia. I have trouble with the sitting for long periods of time. Would it be okay if I am getting up and walking around during class or lying on the floor?"

After the first day, the class settles in for the challenges of the semester: distinguishing between nouns and pronouns, finding the predicate ("What is the meaning of that word, Miss?"), composing the topic sentence, and writing the journal entry. The journal: one thing I have learned is that in this private space of written material, shyness seems to fall away from the students.

Sometimes, like Tanya, they write me stories they heard as children: "In past time the people at the hunting were using some sort of weapon that were prepared from eagle feathers. One day, a strong feeling eagle flew by and . . . ."

They also tell me about their pets: "In my family we have three dogs, a cat two birds and assorted girbals." "The hardest part about coming America is leaving behind my pet yak." "I have not come to school all this week because my cat was ran over. I feel silly but cant stop crying."

Sometimes they tell me their secrets. "Samoans are short and stocky, and I'm no different but I have very large feet—size twelve, I'm a big man inside though, I know it & my feet show it!"

They express their dreams. "No one YET in my family has a college degree; excepting ME who WILL get one, hopfully!?"

And they tell me their fears. "I was adopted, and everybody in my family is smarter then me. I dont want to come to school but want to work for a Search and Rescue team, my folks want me to be a docter tho. I will do it but its hard. Please help with spelling mistaks."

Although I always write comments in the margins, by unspoken agreement I never mention the journal when I'm talking to a student. I feel that I am, perhaps, a little like a priest in a confessional; I exist only as a receptacle for their thoughts.

Once I forgot my role, thinking I could traverse the space between the journal and the real world. I was wrong, however. I walked by the desk of the Samoan man (who had a wonderful sense of humor) and hoping to continue the little joke he had brought up in his journal, I paused and whispered to him, "Size twelve?" He looked up, shocked. I could tell then that he had never consciously connected me, the teacher, with her, the journal reader. How could I know this secret thought? Shaking his head, he turned away from me and went back to his writing.

I had broken the rules. We people in a developmental class look out for each other. We must because those in the class so often behave in extraordinary ways. William, for instance—who had told us his brains were fried—was indeed, as the King of Siam would say, a puzzlement.

William came in every day with a new list of questions he'd been worrying over. "What's a semester? Why isn't *girl* a pronoun? How many prepositions do you have in a sentence?" First I'd have a go at answering his queries, but my words didn't often clarify things for him. Perhaps Tanya, who had been pacing up and down across the back of the room, would stop and write a list of pronouns on the board. Or Beverly would shout out a sentence with no prepositions at all, trying to show him their function. Various other students would then good-naturedly remind him that he'd asked about the word *semester* last week. He would listen carefully and take a few notes each time.

Then would come the next stage of his investigation: "So, a sentence will always have a verb following the preposition?" No one ever ignored him or laughed at him, but we would at last give up for the day and go on to other matters.

William, like Tanya, had difficulty sitting through class, but he didn't walk around the room. He would instead grab his backpack with a terrible rattling of papers and leave abruptly at whatever moment he felt the need, sometimes in the middle of a test, or while a student or I was talking, or even when he himself was explaining work at the board. Someone would always follow him just to make sure he was okay. Usually, he would just be sitting outside the door with his knees hunched up to his chin, collecting himself, and waiting to apologize when everyone came out.

The most tender moment that I ever experienced in a classroom (or perhaps anywhere) came one very rainy morning while I stood at the board circling controlling ideas in topic sentences. Jason, my student with M.S., was not there, and I thought to myself that he probably had not made it because of his physical limitations; he had the use of only one hand.

Then suddenly the door opened and in wheeled Jason, his clothes soaked through and water dripping from his hair. The van which transported him to school had left him off across the street, and he'd propelled himself over in the downpour. He stopped right by me, just inside the door at the front of the room, and gave us all his usual serene old/wise smile.

Quickly José got up and helped him off with his coat; then two young men, without a word, walked out of the room, returning in a minute or two with wads of paper toweling, and—as I continued to talk—they very gently and carefully dried off Jason and his wheelchair. He thanked them with great dignity and got out his papers. I went on explaining a sentence on the board: My father makes great menudo. "Now, which word controls the sentence?" I asked the class.

"*Great*," came the answer—from Jason.

I am always saddened to see the semester end. By this time I've heard all the excuses: "Dear Teacher, I didn't come to class Thurs. becaus I did'nt wont to walk thru the rain puttles." This was another note from Paula Franz (she should have taken a lesson from Jason). Andrea wrote me, "I didn't mak it to class on Tues. Couldn't fine a parking place." From José came: "I can't write today. Please give me another chance." And there is my perennial favorite: "I have missed a month of class but must pass this course, can I do xtra credit?"

I have also lost a third of the people: Andrea and most of the others in the back row have disappeared; Tamad, after much urging and resistance, has transferred to an ESL class ("Please allow my stay. I can make the writing, I am hard worker"); one or two have found jobs and put off their education—probably with a grateful sigh—one more time. But the writing survivors are still there, and it's time for something we call the class pot luck.

Everyone is asked to bring a dish traditional of his or her culture. I always cook up my spicy El Paso chili. We get a mix of food as diverse as the students themselves: hush puppies, Vietnamese spring rolls, papayas splashed with lime, fried zucchini, Irish stew, vegetarian lasagna, Mexican wedding cookies, Russian eggs, chicken McNuggets. People exchange gifts and bring their favorite music. Sometimes we can even get a person like Jerry to play his guitar for us.

But it's never enough. We don't want to let go that last day. People have studied together, found jobs for each other, exchanged baby sitters, gone on camping trips, gotten married—and, from my hopeful perspective, even learned to recognize a preposition and write a paragraph. We feel nostalgic now. All the questions have been asked even if they weren't understandable or answerable. All the papers have been written and re-written and re-written. The trauma of the predicate is behind us. Now, no one wants to put down that last taco and go home. But people push Jason out to his waiting van, give William a hug for good luck, and wave goodbye to all.

This was the best class, I decide as usual, shutting the classroom door behind me. And next semester I'll think of something to keep those people in the back row from quitting.

Young teachers often feel that they get stuck with developmental courses which no one else wants. We "seasoned travelers" know that the students in these classes bring with them a wisdom about life's potential for disaster, a strong desire for information, a surprisingly intense camaraderie and willingness to share, and a deep respect for education. They are a gift to us all. They are why we go on being teachers.

The Meaning of Life

Mitchell Levenberg, St. Francis College

It was Wednesday which meant in-class writing day in my
Developmental 101 class, and the assignment which I wrote on the board
was "Explain the Meaning of Life." The students didn't really have to tell me
what the meaning of life actually is; I had no such expectations, but I did
want them to think about what gave their lives meaning and the moment I
finished writing the question on the board, one student, Joe, called out,
"That's easy — sex!" and then another student named Jerry said, "It depends
what kind! There's SEX and then there's sex!" I thought about how Joe just
kind of reacted to things while Jerry always gave things a little bit more
thought. Then I said, "Just write it down. I want you to write this down and
we'll discuss it later." But then Lana, someone who knew the meaning of
very little, asked, "How are we supposed to know the meaning of life?" And
I said, "You're not," and then Bobby said, "Then why are we doing this?"
and I said, "Just write down what you think the meaning of life is, in other
words, what it means to you." "What what means?" Juan asked. "Life!" I
cried. "Oh," Juan said, "why didn't you say so in the first place?" It went on
like this for a while until Carla asked, "You mean like a house, and a dog and
a husband? That kind of thing?" "Yes," I said. "That kind of thing." "In other
words, like sex!" Joe called out again, and Jerry, sitting right next to him,
said, "Of course that depends on what kind of sex," and I said, "Just write!"
and Lana, complaining, said, "Do we have to write about sex?" And I said,
"No, of course, I mean yes if you. . . ." "Then we have to write about it?"
Samantha asked, and I said, "You don't have to write about anything!" so Joe
said, "Good, then we can leave?" and I didn't bother answering that one and
someone said (I think it was Lana), "This is too hard," and another said, "It's
too boring," and someone else didn't have paper, and someone else a pen,
and the one lending the other one a pen asked, "What color do you want?"
and so on and so forth until finally, twenty minutes into class, they started
writing except for one young pale washed-out student in the back, Richard,
who had been writing all the time and now appeared finished.

No one seemed to notice Richard; no one ever seemed to notice him, and even I sometimes wondered whether he was real or not or perhaps just some insistent figment of my imagination, an apparition from admissions; but nevertheless there he was, day after day, never saying a word but always writing, especially today, with great intensity and purpose that made me want to check his records, his registration form, his birth certificate, even his pulse. And for the next forty minutes, while everyone else wrote, Richard just sat there, staring at me, or, as it really seemed, staring straight through me as if he were trying to figure out the meaning of my life.

What was it with this guy? I wondered. Could it be that he did know the meaning of life? For after all, wasn't it always the most unlikely-looking person who turns out to be the prophet, the holder of life's mysteries? Could it be? Nah, I thought. But maybe . . .

After forty minutes I stopped everybody. "Okay," I said, "who wants to read?" Carla's hand shot up. "Carla?" I asked. "Okay," she said. "The meaning of life to me is a house in the suburbs, two kids, one boy, one girl, my husband, Johnny Depp, and our pet poodle, Puddles." "Poodle?" Joe called out. "I hate poodles!" "Puddles?!" Jerry cried. "What kind of a name is Puddles?" And then Joe said, "If poodles are the meaning of life then I don't want to live anymore!" "It depends what kind of poodle," Jerry said. "There are POODLES and then there are poodles." "Nah," Joe said. "A poodle is a poodle." The class roared. Carla was angry. "It's not just the poodles," she said. "It's the whole package!"

"What about you, Joe?" I asked. "What did you write?"

"Nothin'," Joe said. "Nothin'?" I asked. "You must have written somethin'," I said, speaking his own language, trying to stay in the rhythm of his own speech so as not to lose him. "Nope. Nothin'," he said. "Come on, Joe!" Carla called out to him. "Don't be a chicken!" Well, if there was anything worse for Joe than poodles, it was being called a chicken, so he said, "Okay, okay, but it really sucks." "So it sucks," I said. "Read it anyway."

So Joe read: "The Meaning of Life: What is the meaning of life? Who knows? Who's supposed to know that? If you knew that, you'd lose all the mystery and it's the mystery that makes life worth livin' like going to a club and not knowin' who ya gonna meet if you're gonna meet anyone at all or let's say you do find out the meaning of life by accident let's say and you don't like very much what you find out? Then whaddya do? Kill yourself? Wouldn't it be better to go on in blissful ignorance just having a good time not knowin' nothin' and just kinda letting things happen?"

"Like you! Right, Joe?" Carla called out. "What a cop-out!" But before Joe could answer her, I said, "Oh, I don't think so. It's a perfectly good response to the question. I didn't say you had to have an answer or for that matter even wanted one."

That's when I looked at Richard again and before I realized what was happening, despite a sudden flurry of raised hands, despite students who had never even spoken before wanting to get into the fray, into the great debate on the meaning of life, despite all that, I could focus only on Richard now, because deep down, I was convinced that he might actually know the meaning of life, so I said, "Richard, what about you?" And rather than jolting him out of his trance-like stare, I seemed to have put him into a deeper one.

"Yeah, Richard! What about you!"

"Yeah!"

"Yeah, come on, Richard!" All over the classroom people wanted to hear what Richard thought about the meaning of life, probably because poor Richard didn't really seem to have any life at all or at least any real meaning anyone could attribute to it. In fact, sometimes I wondered whether Richard had ever left his seat since the first day of the semester. Whenever I walked into the classroom he'd already be sitting there, looking bored and impatient as if he had been sitting there a long time, and when the class ended he'd make no attempt to get up, let alone leave when everyone else, including myself, would leave. No, Richard stayed and stayed. He never came; he never left. He just sat there looking as if he never changed his clothes or washed or even ate. Not that things were that way but that they seemed that way was good enough to put ideas in my head about certain divine souls in the guise of ill-dressed, ill-washed and ill-fed developmental writing students.

"Richard!" I said again. "Would you like to let us know what the meaning of life is?" Richard did respond this time, but only by shaking his head no. "Oh, come on!" I said. "Everyone else would like to know." "Yeah!" the class shouted. But he just kept shaking his head from side to side, back and forth, no, no, no, almost as if he had lost control of it, as if he couldn't stop it whether he wanted to or not.

"Are you sure?" I asked. His head kept shaking. Ordinarily, this would be enough for me to just go on to someone else, but somehow it was different this time: no matter how many times he shook his head no, I could not let Richard off the hook. For some reason I needed, wanted, was desperate for Richard to read his essay almost as much, perhaps, as he wanted, needed, and was desperate not to read it. "Yes, Richard," I said, recognizing my own insistent tone, "I'm afraid this time you'll have to read."

And again, he just shook his head no, over and over, and then suddenly it happened. It started with one (Joe, I think) and then another (Jerry, I suppose, after he thought about it for a moment) and then a third and a fourth and suddenly the whole class was chanting his name, "Richard! Richard! Richard!" and the louder they chanted, the more Richard shook his head no. And then there was me, without even realizing it, walking towards him, slowly, hardly discernably really but still moving steadily towards him and the class chanting louder than ever, "Richard! Richard! Richard!" and me saying, over the din, "Come on, Richard, come on!" and he shaking his head no and then me suddenly at his desk, right in front of him, reaching for his paper, the chanting getting louder and louder and my hand getting closer and closer to the edges of his paper until suddenly he grabbed it himself and raised it way above his head while the chanting got louder and for the first time I thought of retreating, of heading back to my desk, of giving up and forgetting the whole thing and restoring order to the class, but I knew it was too late, that I had gone too far, that perhaps I was risking all—my career, my life, my students' lives—for who knows what would happen next, for after all, wasn't it possible that I might be tampering with the untamperable, that there is an inherent risk for those who search for the truth in untrodden and dangerous places such as in the unsuspecting minds of our own students? Yet at the same time wasn't it my job, no matter at what cost, with a little nudging, a little cajoling, a little insistence perhaps, to draw out this hidden truth, to develop it, to help the students reveal it to themselves, to their fellow students, to the world even, and in the most grammatical and rhetorical way possible?

I think it was that very thought that made me grab again for Richard's essay, but again I missed as Richard raised it even higher over his head, even further beyond my reach. The class groaned. Then Richard, sensing perhaps a real fight on his hands, suddenly crumpled the paper into a ball and shoved it into his mouth. "No!" I cried. "No!" the class cried. "It's okay, Richard," I said. "If you don't want to read you don't have to. Just don't swallow it!"

Then the class seemed to break off into two distinct groups. The first, led by Joe, began chanting, "Swallow it! Swallow it!" while the other group, led by Jerry (who might very well have given this too some thought), began chanting, "Spit it out! Spit it out!" As for me, I started to back up, retreat you might say, for now at least, all the way back to my desk.

And it was when I was safely behind my desk again that I turned around and wrote on the board: "For Thursday: In five hundred words or less, 'What if . . . .'" And that's when everyone stopped chanting and started groaning again.

"What if what?" Joe asked. "Exactly! Class dismissed!" I said, glad to have finally restored order. And then, as if nothing out of the ordinary had happened that day, everyone got up, dropped their "Meaning of Life" essays on my desk, and left.

Everyone, of course, except Richard, who with his cheeks still bulging with one essay, immediately began writing the other one. So instead of leaving with all the others, I sat down again behind my desk, just staring at Richard, waiting, and thinking the whole time: "What if . . . what if. . . ."

What I Learned from My Students

Barbara J. Lootens, Purdue University

The April sun filters into my dreams. I lie there, vaguely wondering whether my thoughts of Scott are a continuation of my night-long anxiety or the beginning of a new day. Should I pass him? Can he function in a regular English class? Will he get an instructor who understands him? What if he doesn't? Quietly I leave my sleeping husband, walk into the kitchen, and pour water into the coffee maker. Cup in hand to catch the first dark drops, I remind myself that it's Sunday. I can forget about Scott.

That is not true. I can never forget about Scott, or Shawn, or Lisa, or the hundreds of students I have worried about in a lifetime in the classroom. As I stare out the window, the forsythia, gloriously golden, stabs at my heart. It takes me a moment to trace the source of the pain. I'm leaving them—all of them. After forty-five years, this will be the last spring that a student will disturb my sleep, invading my mind and taking over my life. I will be "retired."

Why the passive voice? I am retiring myself! I study those thoughts. How can I retire myself? What I am is a teacher. I am Barbara, the teacher. A daughter, yes, with a father, thankfully vital and loving in his old age; a wife, yes, with a husband more loving than when I married him; a mother, yes, with children who have brought me nothing but joy; a grandmother, yes, with grandchildren as glowing and golden as the forsythia in my yard. Yet, most of all, I am a teacher.

I can still see my mother and father perched precariously on tiny red chairs as I pass out paper for their spelling tests, and I can still feel the thick pencil in my hand as I draw lopsided stars on the lined yellow sheets to reward my students for getting all the words right. When I close my eyes, I can still hear the thud of the lid of the piano bench as I store their homework and dismiss class. "Time for recess!"

It is time. I know that. I get another cup of coffee and look again at the forsythia and think of Scott. Have I done enough for him? In the two weeks left in the semester, can he straighten out the comma splices? If he doesn't, will his English 101 instructor know that he's making them because he senses that the ideas belong together, not in separate sentences? Will his next instructor learn to admire Scott's courage in trying to remove his learning-disabled badge? Will she find the patience to help him keep trying?

And what about Kevin? Will she know him well enough that he will confide in her about his accident and the coma that left him with no memory of the past? What kind of writing assignments will she give him to help him get over his desire to hide his feelings? Will she learn when to push him and when to remain silent? Will she learn from her students all that she needs to know to teach all my Scotts and Kevins during other springtimes?

I am sure that I did not learn all that I could have learned from Scott and Kevin, but I do know that I have learned more from them and from my other students than I have ever taught them. When I was lucky, I was able to teach them the mechanics that would spare them embarrassment when they were required to write. Perhaps I helped them to organize their thoughts so that others could understand them, and on occasion, I believe that I helped them to learn to respect themselves and have confidence in their own abilities. This was my job, and I did it as well as I possibly could, learning by trial and error as all teachers do. What I did not realize, at least consciously until this moment, was how much my students have shaped me. It was they who made me what I am.

From them, I learned not to make premature judgments about others. First impressions are often not lasting ones, a lesson which must be learned quickly, especially in the teaching of "developmental" students. "These people are losers" is the natural response because, in many ways, they have been losers—neglected, often abused, and always insecure (often with good reason). I think of Alice, middle-aged, overweight, and red-faced. Racing into my classroom late on the first day, she was out of breath and perspiring when she tackled the placement test. When I read her two-page paper, which consisted of equally breathless fragments, exclamations, and complete thoughts punctuated as a single sentence, I knew she was doomed from the start. Later I discovered that after her husband had dropped dead, leaving her with no insurance, she had taken and passed the G.E.D. examination in an attempt to gain the skills to support her two natural and two foster children. Finding that greater training would be necessary, she had enrolled in the university with hopes of earning a degree in education. I cannot truly take credit for what seemed to me to be a miracle, but when her name was called four years later at commencement, I joined in the standing ovation. Now the Director of Basic Education for Adults, which is affiliated with a local public school system, she is the community's leading advocate for higher education.

My pride in the success of Alice and of many others like her is quickly tempered by remembering the failures. Were they all mine? I honestly don't know, but I am compelled to accept some blame. However, I have been forced to learn, though grudgingly, that the ability to accept failure is a slow process which can never be totally completed. Far too many students have taught me that. In the abstract, it is easy to say that not everyone can succeed in developmental courses and that no one is to blame. Whether logical or not, I still hurt when students drop out; when they become belligerent, even hostile; and I hurt even more when they become dull-eyed and apathetic. Then I become angry. I want to shake them and yell, "Learn, damn you! Learn!"

Dealing with the feelings of guilt before they become incapacitating is still difficult for me, yet in my more rational moments, I know that, in order to help the students that I can help, I have to let go of the pain caused by failure. Still, I think of dear, sweet, dense Paulette and wonder, "If I had her today, could I . . . ?"

From my students, I have learned to not give up too easily. I have watched them struggle against odds that I can only try to imagine, revealing more courage and endurance than I ever knew existed. I remember Kurt with the blackened fingernails, who never missed an early-morning class even though it meant coming straight from his fifty-hour-a-week foundry job. I remember Dan, whose grandmother came up with tuition money in defiance of her son who wanted Dan to forget school to "earn an honest day's work." Then there's Rick, recently engaged, who asked for advice on how to encourage his not-yet-born children to be readers so that "they won't go through what I've gone through." And Colleen, whose brain disorder caused "electrical explosions" when she studied too hard or too long at a time, the same Colleen who was recognized at the Honors Convocation. I think again of Scott, who has come so far in such a short time.

Over the years as I have watched my students worry over each other's papers, forgetting themselves as they made suggestions and asked questions, I have grown to understand how much all human beings need each other. I have seen for myself proof of the joy that can come from being involved in another's life when one student celebrated another's success or mourned another's failure and offered to help.

Two weeks from now, when this spring semester ends, I will tell my class goodbye and wish them well. They will smile at me; some will even thank me for what I have done for them. I will watch them leave the room, turning to their friends, unaware that they have given me what I most need for the rest of my life—sure knowledge that love begets love.

My mind races, sifting through the years of faces, of piled-up papers, of disturbed dreams, with a sense of loss strangely mixed with a sense of renewal. Rousing myself, I look again at the forsythia casting its shadow on the greening grass. It's so beautiful, I think. It's spring!

Blind Date:
The Pleasures and Pains of Teaching

Madeleine Murphy, College of San Mateo

Another blind date.

I have done this before, of course, but the sensation is born anew each time. I'm excited. This day has been highlighted in my calendar for months, and the preceding weeks dedicated to its preparation. And I'm *nervous*. My clumsiness betrays this. Trying to move silently out of bed, my foot kicks over a glass of water, my overstuffed briefcase bangs painfully against my knee as I make my way to the kitchen, and I suddenly wish—here on the brink of it all—that I could just lurk unseen, an *eminence grise*, a Mycroft Holmes working through more visible agents. Plus, a rainstorm straight out of the Old Testament is in full rush out there. May the Spirit of the Coffee Tree preserve me.

Insulated from the floods outside by the thick darkness that precedes a winter dawn, I stand before the mirror, my face illuminated from below by the cheap lamp on my dresser. Looking right for my date is essential. A poor first impression will haunt our relationship. I must look friendly, but not endearing; intelligent, but not intimidating; relaxed, but not casual.

From the mirror, Boris Karloff stares back at me. Perhaps I was wrong to believe that four hours' sleep would be enough. I root about hopefully for some makeup, but then remember that I used my one tube of lipstick to write down Scrabble scores in a bar game the previous week.

Now the real challenge begins: dressing right. I have prepared well, having laid out the previous night an array of possible outfits. In the sober darkness, however, none looks right. The black skirt is too short and will put them off; trying to look cute at 8 a.m. is like drinking wine at breakfast, and my date may be intimidated by such eccentricity. The Beavis & Butthead T-shirt will of course be immediately detected for the ingratiating ploy it is, as will the Giants jacket. The suit my mother gave me is certainly mature, but a tad severe; besides, it makes me look like an attorney, which may strike an unhappy chord with a date who's out on parole. A pile of clothes, hastily

149

pulled on and impatiently rejected, grows steadily in the shadowed corner of the room. By the time I am dressed, it's 7:01.

In the half-seen depths of the bed, my partner stirs. "Arra oownmm mm gba," he murmurs. These are sounds from another world, a warm secret world, where a gentle sun moves over a slow softball dream. Perhaps it is time for some impromptu research on the effects of cold water on REM sleep. Anxiety makes me uncharitable.

I am ready. Armed only with twelve pounds of paper and a caffeine buzz, I head outside. The wide blackness, ruffled by wind, soaks me instantly. The sizzle of a distant car skimming the wet road frames the silence. The air smells of wet stone. It occurs to me that I do not know where I parked my car. Panic strikes: I must not, must not, be late for my date; of all of my missteps, this is the worst.

Of course, I am not late. I arrive at the appointed venue, a community college classroom in the San Francisco Bay area, at 8 o'clock sharp. Students mill quietly about in the corridor, waiting, occasionally shouting a greeting to a friend. "Hey, wanna go to the cafeteria after class?" "Nah, I gotta go home and look after my mom." The room looks like every other hideous institutional room—the strip lights glare, the board is dusty, and no one has turned on the heating. I am relieved that I have arrived on time, or as so many like to say, in a timely manner. Unloading my packets of paper at the table, the suave inanity of the phrase suddenly strikes me; surely the action itself is timely, not the manner in which it's performed. Aha! My pulse accelerates slightly: the word light is *on*—the curtain up—the performance in progress. Perhaps I'll raise this interesting semantic point during our relationship. It will depend on the temper of my date. Raising my head, I take a first look.

And here, at last, is my date. Or rather, dates, for there are over thirty of them: an archipelago of human mysteries, stuffed into small wrap-around desks, each surrounded by a neat pile of books, wet coats, thermoses, binders. Basic writing students, most looking for eventual college transfer, some just wanting to brush up their skills, some here as a condition of their parole, others because their parents bribed them with a cherry-red 1993 Toyota Celica. Only a handful are here willingly. Most call this class "Bonehead English" and have had to wangle some compromise with their self-respect. Before the week is out, I will hear the results of these internal negotiations: "I shouldn't really be in this class, but I totally blew the test"; "I hate school, man"; "I write good, but only on stuff that interests me"; "My high school sucked" (this almost always from the wiser students); "Well, I guess we all have to work on skills" (this from the wisest); and my favorite—"English is for chicks," from an ex-gang member whose myriad usage errors could not conceal a sweet lyricism that I envied greatly. For many, life in and out of the classroom has consisted of a series of low-level skirmishes with failure. Success, for most of them, has consisted principally in not drawing attention to their difficulties. If no one realizes they're dyslexic, that their jeans come from Woolworth's, that they never really understood the book they were supposed to write a report on, that they never felt part of the classroom, then they have won—even at the cost of an F. Many are just plain silly. And many have survived experiences which would lay me flat.

But these before me are not their predecessors, but their own selves, unknown even in their familiarity. Their vital presence animates this dead room. Tiny sounds flex like sinews in the silence—anoraks rustling, shoes whispering against the linoleum floor, hitches of breath muffled behind polite fists. The weight of their collective gaze is almost palpable. Over thirty pairs of eyes are trained on me: watchful, guarded but polite, ready to give me a try, but already steeling themselves for the compromise and eventual failure that experience has taught them to expect.

Here is an attentive-looking dark-eyed girl with excellent posture, snappily dressed, lightly made up, a fresh pad of paper on the desk before her. She has already written ENGLISH 801 in purple ink at the top of the page, and decorated the zero with a happy face. She smiles hopefully when I catch her eye. Perhaps she survives the writing ordeal by ingratiating herself with her tormentor. Behind her lurks a boy, about eighteen, his cheek resting on his hand. His desk is empty, his bag is clutched on his lap, and he has not taken off his coat. His thoughts are so clear that they might be written in the air over his head: GET ON WITH IT. Over against the wall, another young man with long hair and a Metallica T-shirt keeps his eyes low. I know already he will never say a word in class. Thin white boys with long hair and Metallica T-shirts never say a word in class. Only I and his immediate friends will ever know that he is wickedly funny. The girl behind him is leaning back slightly in her chair, her arm draped comfortably over the desk, surveying me with good-humored challenge. Her baseball hat is set jauntily backwards, pulled down over the nape of her neck where her delicately braided cornrows are gathered together in a pony-tail. She is waiting for me to screw up, but will not be vindictive when I do. She has learned that we are all screw-ups to some degree. Next to her sits a man of about thirty. He is somewhat uneasy at finding himself amid this sea of teenagers, and masks his discomfort with the air of a judicious consumer, assessing whether or not to buy what I have to sell.

And what do my dates see? To a limited extent, I can guess: a plump white woman, English (or Irish—they are never sure of the accent), funny, good-humored, dressed in the height of thrift-shop fashion, coifed by Supercuts, shod by Woolworth's. A part-time teacher, in other words. Beyond that, I never know. Some see a kind of immigration official, controlling the entry port of Academe. Others seem to think I speak in code, that my random comments are in fact a trail of disheveled clues which when correctly interpreted will lead to *the right answer*—a human CD game. Many see yet another representative of a society they don't think they can penetrate.

Time to break the ice. Each student interviews his or her neighbor and presents that person to the class. A list of biographies begins:

"This is Mike. He's twenty and comes from Burlingame. Let's see: he likes snowboarding, rollerblading, and basically just, you know, hanging out with friends or whatever. He doesn't have a major and he pretty much hates writing, but he wants to improve his skills. Oh yeah, and he really wants a good grade."

"OK, well, this is, um, Cherise—did I say your name right?—she's nineteen and wants to major in broadcasting; she lives with her mom and two brothers, and likes country music, which personally makes me barf, but it's a free country, I guess! [Laughter.] She loves to write, says she writes poetry all the time. And that's it. Oh, and she comes from Manila, but now she lives in Daly City."

"Is it me now? OK. This is Tamsin. She's been a secretary for years and has three kids in high school, which like you'd never guess 'cause she looks about twenty-five to me, but anyway, she wants to get a better job so she's going back to school. She hasn't really done any writing since she was in high school but she says she likes a challenge. Um, what else. We found out we're both really into our church and do a lot of stuff there, which is something in common, and—um—she's a nice person!"

"Thanks, Marie! Well, let me introduce Marie, a very nice young lady from San Mateo. She has a lot of important ambitions: she wants to be a physiotherapist, raise a family, and rebuild classic cars! Although she says she enjoys writing for fun, she doesn't enjoy writing for a grade, but thinks it's important to work on grammar problems. As for hobbies, Marie enjoys listening to music and being with friends."

"Um, yes. This is Frank. He plays baseball for the college, so he's got a pretty full schedule, and he hopes you don't mind if he's late a lot. [Laughter.] What with the baseball and all, he doesn't have too much time for hobbies, but he likes any sports, and used to do, like, skateboarding a lot."

"OK, here's Lily. She's from—I can't read my writing; is that Woodside? OK, she lives in Woodside and likes watching action movies, hanging out with friends, and stuff like that. She's in her second year here and wants to transfer to UC Davis to do biology. And she's twenty-two."

The litany continues: snowboarding, hanging out with friends, movies, Pearl Jam, he doesn't know what his major should be, she's really into animal rights, he wants to improve his writing skills so he can communicate better, she never writes unless she has to. Their real biographies remain hidden: astonishing talents, chilling parental neglect, bonecracking hard work, obstacles overcome, shallow miseries.

Romance does not belong exclusively to mating rituals. This first class meeting, I think, holds all the spice, the awkwardness and exhilaration of the hottest of hot dates. Over the next sixteen weeks, I will see more of these people than of my friends or partner. In certain ways, I will get to know them intimately. They will struggle to recreate their inner lives in the hard, unforgiving medium of print; I will read their writings, try to get into their individual heads to follow their meaning as it emerges, struggle to find the key that will unlock their intellects and begin to set them free. By the end of the semester, we'll have forged that strange, lopsided intimacy that exists between teachers and students. We will cohabit an intellectual terrain, where we talk about gun control, the different ways men and women use conversation, or whether angry rhetoric can indeed be blamed for acts of terrorism. We will discuss writing strategies, dissect writing structures, review written usage. But this academic landscape will be bombed periodically by events in our private lives, too. Grandfathers will die. Cars will be totaled. Flu will ravish the room. My partner will leave me and I will not sleep for a week, lending an intriguing urgency to my teaching style. The cartoon biographies the students have drawn will deepen into full portraits as I am surprised, often humbled, by glimpses of their real lives. A cheerful young woman, whose even temper plants in my mind a picture of a tranquil, uneventful life, writes her final essay describing her recent heart transplant. A class discussion on the nature of despair prompts another merry girl to mention that her fiancé died before her eyes the year before. After a prolonged absence, the class joker listens patiently to my standard lecture about the need actively to take responsibility for his education; in response, he explains that he had been obliged to go to court for custody hearings—his small son, he feels, is not being adequately cared for by his ex-wife. A silent boy hands in a thin, poorly-developed paper, whose margins are decorated with brilliantly crafted drawings. A teenager with a pony-tail, to whom I had been pontificating for much of the term about the importance of facing up to a challenge, reveals one day that she has a pilot's license.

Like any relationship, this one will have its langueurs. Around mid-term, we will both give in temporarily: I beaten down by the relentless tide of errors and glib inanities, they exhausted by relentless prompting for more analysis, more explanation, more work. I will renew my faith by rereading Mina Shaughnessy and drinking plenty of wine. They will renew theirs by skateboarding and by receiving an unexpected A. We will go back to the work, vigorous and excited. Then it will all be over. I'll never really know which ones I was useful to, or which ones I might have held back. I hope most will have learned something: about writing, about themselves, about negotiating the high seas of learning, about planting their private flag in the academic landscape and claiming it as their own. I know they'll have taught dozens of things—things which, as I dart about my bedroom on a cold winter morning looking for clothes, I can't even predict. How many dates can claim as much?

And I know I'll still be just as nervous next time.

My Most Unforgettable Student

Emily J. Schaefer, Hartwick College

On a May afternoon more than ten years ago, the telephone rang in my rural upstate New York home, and my life was irrevocably changed by a student who would be dumbfounded now if he knew that I remember that date, remember that afternoon as if the events of the day had happened a week ago. I picked up the phone that day, and a familiar male voice said, "I have my bike and an extra helmet. Can you come out and play?" I hesitated and then replied, "Mike, graduation was Saturday, and I thought you were long gone." But it was Mike, and he had graduated, but he was not gone because he had not forgotten that he had promised he would take me riding on his motorcycle before he left Oneonta. With knees already starting to tremble, I agreed to ride, gave him directions to my house, and added only that I would have to be home in time to make dinner for my husband and children.

When I hung up the phone, I looked in the mirror and saw a blue-eyed woman in her forties who had spent too much of her life playing it safe, a woman who had been raised by law-abiding, God-fearing parents to envision clearly and horrifyingly the negative consequences of every rash action. I had given up a biology major at my father's insistence that it was no field for a woman, had married the first man who showed a serious interest in me, and had stayed married to him despite his increasing abuse and the growing neuroses which made him isolate himself and me more and more from our families and former friends.

In the few years before that afternoon, I had been making some progress: at thirty-two I had learned to drive; at thirty-three I started wearing contact lenses; and at thirty-five, when my son started kindergarten, I had gone back to school. It had taken me seven years to finish my degree, but before I finished, I began teaching in the college's writing center. I was still a reticent person, protecting my fragile ego and hiding the decay of my marriage behind a thick wall of reserve and a determination to preserve the illusion of the beautiful family. Whenever an opportunity to break free, even for a day, presented itself, I said to myself, "I can't do that. I'm afraid of the consequences."

But that May afternoon, in response to Mike's invitation, I said an unequivocal "Yes, yes, I can go riding!" I had about twenty minutes until he would be there, and I whirled through my house, thoughts jumbling through my brain: "What do I wear on a motorcycle?" "Where will we go?" "Shall I leave a note for my husband and children?" "What can I possibly say in it?" And then I went into the bathroom and washed my hair.

I had been working with Mike for three years. He had been assigned to me in the writing center after having driven both Helen and Pat, who was afraid of him, to despair of his ever making any progress because of his erratic attendance, unruly appearance, and rude behavior. When Glenn, the center director, assigned him to me, he said, "I'm not doing this because I hate you; I'm doing it because. . . , well, you'll find out." And then he smiled. I guess he had been doing more eavesdropping than I realized on some of my more unconventional conferences with other recalcitrants. So I had never seen Mike, knew of him only by reputation when he came hurtling through my office door, late for his first conference, and dropped a crumpled wad of papers on my desk. I just sat and looked at him and tried not to smile as I said to myself, "This one will not be a problem." But then none of them ever had been, really. They had taught me about ice hockey, macrobiotics, and choosing sneakers; about alcohol, drugs, and outwitting the police; and I was about to learn something new yet again.

Michael Cory Lesser. He was small, maybe 5′6″, dressed in jeans with holes and a black leather jacket, and he had hair, a tangled mass of dark red curls, darker than the red of his beard and moustache and an odd contrast to his veiled, amber eyes. And despite his shuttered look, I fell in love with him at first sight. We made a contrast all right: I, a former homemaker, Cub Scout den mother, baker of cookies and knitter of mittens, a seasoned survivor; he, a racer of motorcycles, a rock climber, rugby player, skateboarder, bent on self-destruction. What he knew about was motorcycles, and what he wanted to write about was motorcycles: buying, racing, wrecking, rebuilding them and buying them again. So I let him. He wrote quite well actually, had been sentenced, according to him, to do time at the writing center because his composition teacher made him write essays about the "Joys of Jello," or "anything bigger than a bread box." She had a reputation too, and Mike had not heard it in time. She gave pending grades which she seldom removed so that students struggled term after term for their first year to their last to rid themselves of Julia Whitter's pending grades and sometimes graduated with them still on their records.

Mike never tired of talking about his machines and his weekends spent careening along Route 80, a narrow, winding, smoothly paved road west of Cooperstown. One day in the middle of our discussion of an unusual departure from essays about bikes and biking to an essay written from the point of view of his black and white cat, Kodachrome, he paused and pulled me to the window to admire his new red Kawasaki GPZ 550, and not too many weeks later he wrote an essay he called "Death of a GPZ" as once again he had escaped serious injury while leaving his machine lying over a stump at the side of the road with its wheels still spinning.

Mike fascinated and mystified me. As a college student he was fearless and suspicious, a risk-taker who was unhappy with himself and what he was doing: majoring in management to please his father, who he thought cared more about his half-brother Billy than he did about him. Billy had the clothes, the car, the fancy school.

One day after I had known Mike for a few weeks, he came in and sat down, and when I looked at him, I realized I was looking into the direct gaze of eyes that were no longer veiled. Other changes followed that had nothing to do with the academic aspects of the twice-weekly half-hours we spent discussing his writing: He was on time. He was well dressed. Eventually, much to my dismay, he cut his hair. As one term ended, and his pending was not removed, he came back. For three years off and on he enrolled in my minitutorial, and for three years I saved space in it for him until the last minute. He eventually quit writing about motorcycles and started writing about books, movies, and philosophy. He asked me to recommend books for him to read. He sent me postcards from winter jobs as a ski-lift operator in Vermont and summer biking jaunts through the Midwest.

But this past Saturday Mike had graduated. I had been near the college that day, picking up my daughter from a swim-team practice, and as I had driven out of town, I had mused to myself that he was gone, that I would miss him, that the "ungrateful wretch" had not taken me riding on his machine after all. No matter, I would have been terrified anyway. He was writing well, and he had been accepted at Clarkson for an engineering program. It was time for him to go, time for me to make some decisions about my own life and the lie of the happy family I had been living for many years, afraid of risking change.

But now I knew Mike was not yet gone; he was on his way to my house, and so I settled on my jeans with the little woven-in red checks, a red shirt, my sturdiest sneakers, and my jeans jacket. And I was writing "Gone biking with a student, be back before dinner" on a scrap of paper to leave on the fridge when I heard his bike come up the long narrow drive. I went outside, and he really was there, unfastening a helmet from the back of the beautiful red, rebuilt Kawasaki. He grinned at me sheepishly and put the helmet on my head, fastened the catch, telling me I looked cute. Cute? No one had ever called me that before. And I thought to myself that as long as I was about to die, I might as well look cute as I was doing it. He suggested Cooperstown, helped me onto the bike, showed me the pegs for my feet, and we were off.

I clutched his leather jacket and fixed my eyes on the tufts of red hair at the base of his helmet, and I soon realized that I trusted him to keep me safe.

As we rode up the long hills and down into the wooded valleys, gradually my fear melted into exhilaration as I breathed the air, now warm, now in the valley cool. There were wild flowers along the road, and my feet were only inches from the pavement. I had never felt so vulnerable, nor so free. Too soon, we pulled up in front of the Bold Dragoon on Pioneer Street, and as we got off the bike, Mike said, "At first I thought you were cold, and then I realized you were scared," and I knew he had felt my knees shaking against his thighs as we rode. We bought a bottle of wine, and we sat in the grass in the park at the end of the lake. We played with some mallard ducklings, and we talked, but what we said I no longer remember. Then it was time to be back for dinner. The ride seemed short, and all I could think of was that I needed to remember this day, this moment, the fresh green leaves, the fragrances, the feel of the leather, the color of his hair, and the sound of the bike.

As we roared up the drive, I could see my husband sitting on the patio, reading the *New York Times*. He looked up as we got off the bike, and I said, "Richard, this is Mike." He nodded, looked down and continued to read. Mike pulled me behind the van in the driveway, put his arms around me, kissed me and said, "I told you I'd come, and I did. Now I'm telling you I'll be in touch." He put on his helmet, fastened the strap, and I gave him one last hug, kissed him on the chin, and he was gone.

I stood in the driveway for a moment, watching him disappear down the dusty dirt road, and then I went into the house, took the note off the refrigerator, wiped my eyes, and began to prepare dinner. I was back, but in actuality I never came back.

I have not been the same since that day. Mike did go to Clarkson and wrote, long, sometimes funny, sometimes wise, sometimes disturbing letters to me in which he poured out his frustrations, his hopes, and his fears, letters I answered late at night from my upstairs room, wrestling with how to encourage him when I knew that my own life was a sham, that nothing I had envisioned of marriage had anything to do with my own life except for the joy I had found in raising my children and the increasing satisfaction I was finding in working with students and their writing. He graduated as an engineer with a minor in technical writing, and this time, unlike two years earlier, his father was at his graduation.

Not long after Mike left Clarkson, I bought a motorcycle of my own, a black and gold Kawasaki LTD 440, a café bike with curly handlebars and a step-seat, and painstakingly I learned to ride. And as I flew along the country roads, I found the strength to make myself vulnerable, to take risks. In fairly quick succession I found a more responsible position at a different college, left my husband of twenty-five years, helped my children through college, took up sailing, rollerblading, and horseback riding. And with each change, each risk, my terror became exhilaration, and the walls of my reserve came down. I wished Mike were there to meet the person I had become.

From time to time I heard from Mike, always when I least expected to. He was working in New York City, not liking the job, not liking the city in which he had grown up. If there was a return address, I wrote back. I tried to tell him how he had influenced me to change my life, but he never really understood.

It has been five years now since I have heard from Mike. But the most recent card came from Italy, and he had begun to live the mountain-climbing adventures he had dreamed of. My life has settled into the life I envisioned as a young woman. I no longer have my Kawasaki, but in May when I have reason to roam the back roads, looking for fiddleheads or a place to fish, I remember that day, that moment, the fresh green leaves, the fragrances, the feel of the leather, the color of his hair, and the sound of the bike.